Beat the Odds in Forex Trading

Founded in 1807, John Wiley & Sons is the oldest independent publishing company in the United States. With offices in North America, Europe, Australia, and Asia, Wiley is globally committed to developing and marketing print and electronic products and services for our customers' professional and personal knowledge and understanding.

The Wiley Trading series features books by traders who have survived the market's ever changing temperament and have prospered—some by reinventing systems, others by getting back to basics. Whether a novice trader, professional, or somewhere in-between, these books will provide the advice and strategies needed to prosper today and well into the future.

For a list of available titles, please visit our web site at www.Wiley Finance.com.

Beat the Odds in Forex Trading

How to Identify and Profit from High Percentage Market Patterns

IGOR TOSHCHAKOV

WILEY

John Wiley & Sons, Inc.

Published by John Wiley & Sons, Inc., Hoboken, New Jersey.
Published simultaneously in Canada.

For general information on our other products and services or for technical support, please contact our Customer Care Department within the United States at (800) 762-2974, outside the United States at (317) 572-3993 or fax (317) 572-4002.

Wiley also publishes its books in a variety of electronic formats. Some content that appears in print may not be available in electronic books. For more information about Wiley products, visit our web site at www.wiley.com.

Library of Congress Cataloging-in-Publication Data:

Toshchakov, Igor, 1961–
    Beat the odds in Forex trading : how to identify and profit from high percentage market patterns / Igor Toshchakov.
        p.   cm.—(Wiley trading series)
    Includes index.
    ISBN-13: 978-0-471-93331-1 (cloth)
    ISBN-10: 0-471-93331-7 (cloth)
    1. Foreign exchange market.   2. Foreign exchange futures.   3. Speculation.   I. Title.   II. Series.
    HG3851.T67   2006
    332.4'5—dc22

                                                    2006004906

Printed in the United States of America.

10 9 8 7 6 5 4 3 2 1

Contents

Introduction

I believe an aspiring trader who applies the principles of this book will save two or three years of practical education in the real market and at least $20,000 of investment capital.

Over the period of time that I have been dealing with speculative currency trade, I was lucky enough to have an opportunity not only to accumulate significant personal experience, but also to observe the work of several hundred independent traders. In addition, I have more than a decade of experience in teaching the theory and practice of currency trading to individual investors. I have also been studying the experience of other traders personally, via books and other publications as well as through participating in discussions at various professional seminars and forums, and have corresponded with traders/colleagues from many countries around the world. This additional experience has allowed me to conduct my own comprehensive research on problems that all serious traders run into during their professional careers. I have also been able to gather extensive material that has served as the initial base for this course and that I have used to create my own trading method. Although nothing ideal exists in nature, I believe my method of trading deserves some serious consideration by those who chose speculative currency trading as a profession or just as a source of additional income.

I would like to start the introduction to this book by mentioning that my own experience as a FOREX speculative trader, and the experience of my respected colleagues whom I have met personally or through publications, has shown that the problems all individual traders have to deal with are virtually the same. However, the number of solutions to the problems is almost the same as the number of traders themselves. Over time, practical results can range from complete triumph to complete desperation. For each participant, this business starts with a variation of a famous line from Shakespeare's Hamlet: "To be a trader or not to be." Is it worth risking money, time and sometimes even a career built in another profession, in order to reach success in a new field? If you join this market, how do you enter into that desirable 5 to 7 percent of participants who statistically succeed? How do you reach success so that the money, time, and energy invested into this business will not only be justified but will also bring you significant dividends? Each participant should be able to answer these questions personally; my task is more modest. For those who have already made the choice in favor of "to be," I offer my version of the secret about how to beat the odds and win the market game. I truly believe this book will allow novice traders to save a good deal of time and money that otherwise would be wasted by following the traditional trial-and-error method of learning from their own mistakes before gaining the necessary experience.[1]

---

[1]Please also note that basic trading terminology, technical analysis terms, graphs, commonly known symbols, and abbreviations related to currency trading have been used in this book without detailed explanations of their meanings. Such information (if needed) could easily be obtained from numerous textbooks and Internet sources, including my own web site at www.igrokforex.com.

PART I

Recommendations to Novice Traders

Before conducting his first transaction on the real FOREX market, novice traders should spend some time familiarizing themselves with this business, learning and also psychologically preparing for participation in real trading. This initial stage can be divided into five steps:

1. Theoretical preparation and learning.
2. Choosing and acquiring the charting and analytical software, and sources of current market information (data vendors).
3. Developing practical skills and using acquired theoretical knowledge; developing trading techniques and skills as well as trading strategies and systems, on the virtual trading account under real market conditions.
4. Choosing the dealer or the broker company.
5. Defining the size of the investment capital and opening a trading account.

You should understand that the learning process could be more effective and mutually enjoyable if you accept some of my preliminary advice and recommendations. These tips are related to the preliminary self-training that you have to conduct so you can better absorb the learning material. Therefore, the first part of the book is focused on general recommendations for novice traders.

CHAPTER 1

How to Get Started

The largest part of the theoretical materials regarding the FOREX market—including the main aspects of the theory of fundamental and technical analysis and also the general information—is not included in this book. The theory of speculative currency trading can be studied using the existing special literature. Before starting to study my trading method, you must familiarize yourself with basic issues of the business in which you are attempting to participate or are already participating. Because my trading method is different from the others that I call traditional ones, the theoretical preparation for my students has to have a specific character. For preliminary preparation on the trade theory, I recommend studying the following four issues:

1. History and development of the FOREX market.
2. Currency market participants, their roles and mutual relationships in the process of trade.
3. Technology and terminology of speculative currency trade.
4. General principles of fundamental and technical analysis.

The main efforts should be focused on studying the technical analysis key issues. The main focus should be on the following two subjects: Support and Resistance Theory and Retracement Theories (Dow and Fibonacci). My method uses only a relatively small part of the general theory of technical analysis and virtually does not employ fundamental analysis at all. However, I do not think it will hurt you to gain some knowledge of subjects that you

3

will most likely not need in the future. On the contrary, this knowledge should help you not just with better understanding of the offered method but internal market tendencies as well.

INFORMATION, DATA FEED, AND TECHNICAL SUPPORT

I don't have any special or particular requirements for computer software, charting programs, or data sources of real time and delayed market quotes and other data. Moreover, my trade method requires only minimal data means. That's why any service (even the cheapest one) delivering real-time market data might be sufficient. It has to have the ability to create charts, a set of main technical indicators, and a minimum set of graphic tools for drawing trend lines, support, and resistance lines. As far as I know, such a service can even be received at no charge from some Internet sites. Long-term analysis requires more sophisticated software, which can be found today on the market at a relatively inexpensive price and with quite acceptable quality.

I didn't do any special research on this subject and cannot offer you a comparison analysis of today's informative services and charting programs. I just want to mention that for the purpose of analysis of long-term charts, including daily, weekly, and monthly charts, I'm using SuperCharts by Omega Research and data feed of the Bridge/CRB. This software doesn't envisage any real-time mode, and the data is loaded from Bridge/CRB daily at 11:00 P.M. GMT, after the end of each trading day. I am entirely satisfied with this service; it fulfills the requirements of my trade method, and I recommend something similar for your usage.

DUMMY TRADING

Before making the final decision to participate in real trade in the FOREX market, the majority of beginners go through the learning stage called dummy trading. This presents a virtual market game, with only virtual capital at risk. Mainly, this is the stage when a newcomer makes a final decision about whether to participate in real trading. His final decision is usually based on the results of such dummy trading. Considering such a training method as a necessary element for the beginners, I must emphasize that the results received in virtual dummy trading are different from the real results of the same traders in the real market when someone deals with real capital. The differences are always not in favor of the real trade. The psychological factor is mostly responsible for this. The risk of losing real money influences the trader in the most negative way, triggering errors, some of which he was successfully avoiding while trading his dummy account. Therefore, I would like to warn you not to be very hopeful and overexcited if the results of working in the real market entirely coincide with the results received in dummy trading. The negative factor built into the trader's psychology will reveal itself anyway. In order to reach a positive result in real trading, you must develop methods of lowering the psychological loads in the stressful situations of real trading. Doing so will constantly train and strengthen your psyche.

The majority of FOREX dealer and broker companies today offer online trading, which presents an optimum solution and a big advantage for the majority of independent traders. Most of those companies also allow virtual dummy trading. In this regard, I have only one recommendation: It would be better to have a dummy trading account with a dealer or a broker you are planning to work with when starting real trading. This way, you generally will be able to evaluate the quality of the service; get used to the manner in which your orders are filled by the dealer; and get used to the peculiarities of this particular on line trading software. If you can independently determine the initial amount of the virtual account, it is desirable for this amount to match the size of the real investment you have planned. Such an approach will allow you to achieve the closest proximity to the real situation you will soon have to deal with.

CHAPTER 2

Establishing a Trading Account

FOREX market has some certain specific characteristics; without knowing them and taking them into consideration, the eventual success in speculative operations could be doubtful.

After the preliminary preparation stage is fulfilled and you think you are ready to participate in real trade in the FOREX market, you must choose a broker or dealer company to conduct your investment operations. You must also determine the size of the initial investment that you will have to transfer into the trade account opened with the chosen dealer company. (Criteria for choosing the dealer company are presented in Chapter 3). As is well known, this market has few specific characteristics; without considering them, success in speculative operations is doubtful.

Unfortunately they are totally beyond the trader's control. Those peculiarities result from conditions characterizing the FOREX market and from historically developed practices and rules followed by all the participants. Some specifications on the FOREX market include high volatility of main currencies; the possibility of trading under conditions of low-interest margin; and relatively high minimum contract value. These conditions are initially considered to be advantages and mainly attract investors into the business. However, they also have a negative side and can be considered as an additional source of risk for a trader. Everything depends on the point of view of the observer, as in the well-known example of the half-empty and half-full glass.

I don't have any doubts that, because you have made the decision to participate in the market, you are sufficiently informed about its advantages. My task is to point out some hidden risks and dangers. Some mistakes made mainly by novice traders during the first stage of their careers are described below. They are connected with insufficient initial capital or its incorrect distribution and management. First, the beginner should be warned about two possible mistakes that are typical and usually made at the very beginning of the trading career.

UNDERCAPITALIZATION RISK

Insufficient initial capital invested into trade is the first mistake made by a majority of newcomers, and it often turns out to be their last mistake.

I have witnessed many cases of full loss of capital invested into currency operations during the first month, weeks, days, and even hours. The invested capital is lost before a novice trader has time and an opportunity for learning.

This happens for a few key reasons. At the beginning of a career, a new trader has neither sufficient knowledge and experience nor the feeling of danger or risk limit that should not be surpassed. Also, at the very beginning, there are some errors that could be avoided with the proper set up before conducting business. One of the frequent initial mistakes is insufficient investment in trading operations. Consider the condition when the average daily oscillation amplitude of the main currency in a percent ratio is comparable to the margin offered to the currency investor by banks, dealers, and brokers. (It is common nowadays to provide the trader with such a condition when the initial margin does not exceed 2 to 4 percent of the size of the contract for the daily trade.)

If the currency oscillates 1 to 1.5 percent on a daily average, the loss of a larger part or even the entire trading account within just a couple of days is possible. I must mention that most novice traders partially realize risks they will have to deal with on the currency market, but are not always capable of precisely formulating and evaluating them. Therefore, they often undertake incorrect actions for lowering them. Logical thinking dictates that the simplest way of lowering the risk of potential losses is by investing the minimum possible amount into trade. At the same time, the idea and the plan are to increase the investment later as the necessary experience, knowledge, and skills are acquired. From my experience, this approach to lower the risk is virtually ineffective and even harmful. The situation reminds me of one of my favorite anecdotes: A commission arrives in a psychiatric hospital to inspect the facility. The commission members see an empty swimming pool into which the patients are diving from the diving board. The commission members ask one of the patients why they are diving into an empty pool. The patient answers that the hospital administration promised to fill the pool with water immediately after the patients learn how to dive.

Usually, most novice traders partially realize the risks they will have to deal with on the currency market, but they are not always capable of precisely formulating and evaluating these risks.

In the same way, many novices try to lower the risk of losses while they are expecting to acquire sufficient practical experience, in order to invest larger amounts later on. They don't understand that a small trading account actually increases the risk of losses. By artificially decreasing the initial investment capital, it is impossible to lower the risk. This is because the size of the trading account and the risk degree of losing some part of the investment capital are not proportionally related. I will illustrate this statement with a simple example. Let's assume there are two accounts. One of them has invested capital of $5,000 and the other $50,000. All other things being equal (such as minimum contract size of $100,000), the initial margin equals 4 percent, and during one trade only, one minimum contract is operated. It is clear that only after two or three unsuccessful transactions (each resulting in a loss of an average of $1,000), the smaller account is practically inoperable and requires replenishment in order to continue participation in the market. See Figure 2.1.

The larger account in this situation remains absolutely sufficient for further operations. Restoring the loss is easier than in the small account. Equalizing the chances to win with large and small accounts is possible only by proportionally decreasing the minimum contract size for a small account owner, or by the same proportional limitation of loss size. It is practically impossible to accomplish either of these options.

The size of the trading account and the risk degree of losing some part of the investment capital are not proportionally related.

The minimum contract size for everyone who works with a good dealer should not be below $100,000. It can be said that this amount is a minimum standard for small individual transactions. By putting short and tight stops, the trader increases the chances the stops will be triggered more often and the total loss will consist of many small losses.

Sometimes, novice traders gradually add money to the trading account. By replacing the losses on the market, they keep the small account instead of immediately investing the large sum in order to lower the risk. As a result, considerable amounts are often lost, invested into the market in small portions. One of the main reasons for these losses is insufficient capital at the moment when it is most required. Therefore, the most frequent disadvantage is insufficient initial investment.

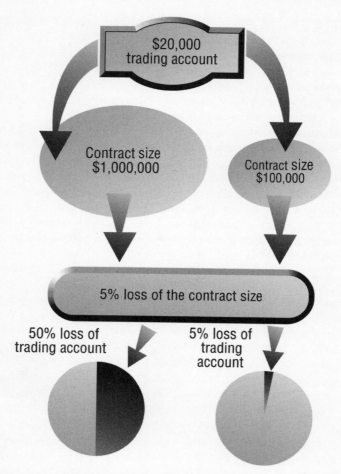

FIGURE 2.1 In this example, the small account becomes inoperable and needs replenishment after a loss of 60 percent of the investment capital. The actual capital losses were equal to just less than two average daily ranges on major currencies. At the same time, the larger account, after having the same capital loss, remains in good and tradable condition.

Recommendation

The trading account (to the degree possible) should be sufficiently large, in order to correspond with market conditions and provide the required security and flexibility in making trade decisions. The trading account is a working tool for the trader. It should correspond not only to those tasks that each trader sets for himself personally, but also to those business requirements under which he will have to work. It is not worth trying to lower the risk by artificially decreasing the initial invested capital. This target should be achieved in a natural way—primarily by trading the contracts of the minimum possible size at each given moment, until the time when the trader acquires sufficient experience and self-reliance.

The trading account is a working tool for the trader, and it should correspond also to those business requirements under which it will have to work.

OVERTRADE RISK

The second mistake made by a majority of newcomers can be attributed to the overtrade risk. This problem is sometimes directly connected to insufficient trading capital. Quite often, though, the problem does not have any relation to this. Rather, it can be explained by the trader's lack of knowledge of the main principles of money management, which means insufficient ability to control someone's trading capital. A trader's trading capital is his tool designed to earn money. In the first place, the trader has to take care to keep this tool intact, because its loss or damage will immediately result in the inability to continue his trading operations.

YOU MUST DETERMINE THE LIMITS OF YOUR RISK IN ADVANCE

Overtrade most often reveals itself when the trader (hoping to receive the maximum possible profit) acquires an oversized contract, risking the larger part of his trading capital in just a single transaction. In case a market starts moving against the trader's position, possible losses can exceed the acceptable limit. The result can be irreparable damage to the working

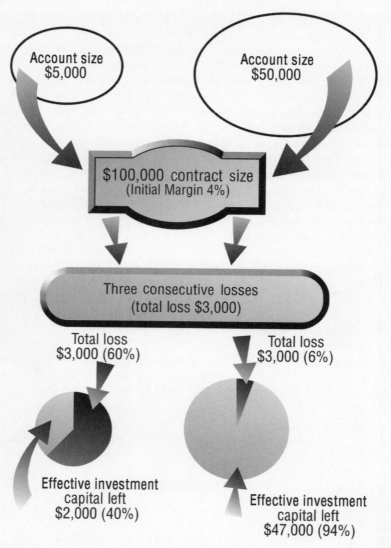

FIGURE 2.2 After a single trade on the full margin (using the maximum leverage), the first trader has lost 50 percent of his total capital. Now he needs to make 100 percent gain on his capital left, just in order to break even. The trader of the second account did not exceed the risk limit and, after suffering the same loss in terms of pips, he still has a quite operable account.

capital, bringing the trading account to a condition unusable for further trade. The account will be unusable in a timely manner in the future, due to the impossibility of covering those losses that occurred during just one transaction. Under current conditions, many banks and dealers offer their clients margin trading terms at a leverage ranging from 20:1 to 50:1 (and even higher). The initial margin as an industry's average is only 2 to 5 percent. Considering the average market activity during one day, it is easy to lose half or even a larger part of the trading capital. In order to avoid this occurrence, it is desirable to use certain margin self-limitation and not to use more than 5 to 10 percent of the trading capital during one trade. Traders should establish their individual limitation for the margin, and possibly keep this limitation not below 10 to 20 percent as compared to the size of the trade contract. In other words, for each $10,000 to $20,000 of the size of your trading capital, only one contract of $100,000 should be traded at any time. See Figure 2.2.

This is the minimum for a majority of the dealers. More details on the problem of overtrade will be presented in Chapter 11.

Recommendation

From the very beginning, it is useful to remember that there is no capital so large that it is impossible to lose during speculative operations in the FOREX market. The risk of losing part of or the entire investment capital is always present where there is the possibility to earn. The currency market is not an exception to this rule. In order to earn, the trader must take the risk of loss. In risking, though, traders must determine in advance the limits of their risk. They should never risk all or the largest part of their trading capital at once. They should risk only that part whose loss they are sure will not result in catastrophic consequences for their trading accounts and the resulting inability to further participation in trading.

CHAPTER 3

Choosing the Right Dealer

After a positive decision is made to participate in speculative trading in the FOREX market, a newcomer should first choose the dealer for conducting a trade. The right choice greatly influences the final success of the whole enterprise. Nowadays, the market is overcrowded with companies and banks offering their services to individual traders and investors to access the currency market. It is not easy to make the right choice without a certain set of criteria. These criteria best correspond to the interests, preferences, and means of each individual trader, and to the trade strategy and tactics chosen by him.

The best way to find the right dealer is to compose a list of questions to ask the dealer, before making a final decision in favor of the preferred company or bank. The following are suggested questions that should be answered by the dealer before you make the decision to open a trading account. Included are my recommendations about the optimization of market operation conditions:

WHAT IS THE AMOUNT (VALUE) OF THE INTRADAY AND OVERNIGHT MARGIN AND CORRESPONDING LEVERAGE?

Many reliable dealers (especially those who offer Internet trading) restrict the margin by 2 to 5 percent, which provides money contract leverage between 20:1 and 50:1. Such terms seem quite reasonable and acceptable, considering the risk/investment efficiency ratio. Higher margin requirements yield lower investment efficiency, whereas a lower margin means that the dealer bargains against his own clients and will do everything possible to prevent his clients from winning. It is difficult to work under such terms because you will confront even more trading problems.

WHAT IS THE MINIMAL CONTRACT SIZE?

Today, a minimal contract size of $100,000 is common for most dealer companies offering their services to individual traders. This contract size is quite affordable from all points of view. It allows traders to conduct reasonably effective money management with limited capital. It also makes it possible for small individual investors to participate in money speculation. Finally, it is a reasonable compromise between the required minimal deposit amount and potential profit level in absolute money nomination.

WHAT ARE THE REQUIREMENTS FOR THE OPERATION ACCOUNT SIZE (MINIMUM DEPOSIT)?

Evidently, the more the investment capital, the easier, safer, more flexible and more effective should be its management. The investment and financial means of traders differ. It is a common situation when somebody willing to participate in speculative trading in a currency market simply does not have enough funds to open an account corresponding to the required safety rules. Each trader has his or her own security level, but I think (although it is a debatable issue) that the operable account size for the individual speculative trader begins with a minimal amount of $30,000, assuming that the initial margin is 2 percent and the minimal contract size is $100,000. I think $30,000 is the required minimum amount corresponding to FOREX market conditions, considering the following:

- If trading a single minimal contract of $100,000, a trader loses a pip amount equal to an average daily swing corresponding to $600 to $1,000 (depending on the selected currency pair), then the loss of 2 to 3 percent of the account per single transaction is rather painless. This loss cannot ruin the account, even in the case of a few consecutive losses.
- Traders must consider that the market "noise" amplitude approximates the amplitude of the average daily exchange rate fluctuation. Therefore, setting shorter stops while trading on a medium or longer

term is unreasonable, because these stops can be offset by incidental oscillation ticks.

- Some trading strategies recommended in this course suggest position reversal and doubling the contract size at the same time, which demands some additional margin for the safety of the corresponding working capital.
- Traders should take into consideration that the trader's job should be adequately reimbursed, including psychological stress, time, and effort spent. There is no reason to spend up to 14 to 16 hours per day trading if you can earn the same money in a less stressful job. Simple calculation shows that even doubling of trading capital in one year can provide you with a secure income, but only in the case of an adequate initial investment.

WHAT ARE THE TERMS OF SETTING AND EXECUTING STOP AND LIMIT ORDERS?

The ideal option is considered to be a transaction execution of stop and limit orders at a fixed price, regardless of the state of the market, its speed, and its direction at the moment. Some dealers guarantee this method of execution, whereas others reserve the right to fulfill an order with a slippage. The value of this slippage depends on the current state of the market, and can fluctuate from a few pips to tens of pips. The slippage evidently creates favorable conditions for abuse of a trader by the dealer, although it is practically impossible to arbitrate the price received from the dealer executing this transaction.

WHAT IS THE SPREAD SIZE AND ITS DEPENDENCE ON THE CONTRACT SIZE?

The spread is the difference between the "bid" and the "ask" prices given at any moment on the trading terminal. The smaller the spread is, the better it is for the trader. The dealer's spread size of five pips at the minimal contract size of $100,000 in a steady market can be regarded as adequate and acceptable, because it does not exceed the 5 percent limit of average daily deviation of currency rates. Some dealers, when trading contracts of $500,000 or more, do offer a spread of less than five pips to their clients. If you do not plan to trade contracts of $500,000 or more, you have to find a dealer who can maintain the minimum spread provided for the contract—even under active and quickly changing market conditions.

WHAT IS THE OPPORTUNITY FOR ON-LINE TRADING USING THE INTERNET AND ADDITIONAL SERVICES: ANALYTICAL, DATA, NEWS, QUOTES, GRAPHICS, AND SUCH?

Many dealers now offer the opportunity for on-line trading, and more will do so in the future. Internet trading has certain advantages over the traditional telephone communication with a broker or a dealer. The main advantages of on-line trading are:

- The opportunity to monitor market movements by following current real-time prices, graphics, and even news on a PC monitor. Usually, it is free and is included in the service and trading software offered by a dealer.
- Dealer trading software as well as other options often provide the trader with the opportunity to manipulate, modify, and customize graphics; conduct technical analysis using indicators; and draw trend lines, support, and resistance lines. In addition to being convenient, this provides substantial money savings. It eliminates the necessity of buying an expensive market-quotes service, and analytical and charting software for conducting technical analysis.
- Internet trading is supported by safe electronic registration data, which provides the necessary security and lowers the possibility of conflict situations between a trader and a dealer. These conflicts are due to probable human errors and slips of the tongue, which are common during live phone communications.

IS IT NECESSARY TO PAY COMMISSIONS AND OTHER PAYMENTS AND DUES?

The most reputable dealer companies charge no commissions for transactions executed by their clients. Others charge some commissions, but usually not very high ones. Personally, I cannot excuse some dealers charging so-called storage fees. In the financial world, the *client* is usually paid when he stores his money—not the dealer. Reputable dealers transferring an open position to the following day execute the rollover operation in accordance with the current LIBOR rates and reflect it in a daily statement.

Depending on the currency pair and direction in which the position was opened at the moment of its transfer to the next day, the client could actually win as a result of the transfer. A certain amount would be added to his account just for holding the position open for more than one day.

Other dealer companies do not bother themselves with such calculations but simply charge the client for the interest on the position transferred to the following day. There are numerous discussions about the possibility of holding two opposite positions open when both long and short positions exist simultaneously. At a dealer's statement in such case, both positions are shown to exist in reality. Each one generates profit and/or loss, and in such form they could be transferred to the following day. I have met a few traders whose manner of trading envisaged such a condition or who used it as an important part of their trading strategy.

I think such arguments are useless and senseless. The positions cannot voluntarily be divided into new and liquidation—depending on a trader's will. The market functions in accordance with certain rules, and it is arranged in such a manner that positions of the opposite tendencies for the same currency pair and of the same size are offset automatically. The spot part of the FOREX market provides the offset and self-liquidation of all open positions by the end of each trading day. At the beginning of the next day, only those positions are recovered that had not been offset due to the lack of opposite (with opposite sign) transactions of corresponding size. For example, if the trader during the day executed USD/CHF transactions for the total amount of $600,000 to buy and $400,000 to sell, then the long USD/CHF position for the remaining $200,000 would be transferred to the next day. As you can see, this is accompanied by the offset of the opposite positions, and the corresponding gain/loss was deposited into or deducted from the trader's account.

There is a simple reason that some dealers allow and even encourage their clients to keep opposite positions for longer than one day. A dealer company can charge interest for practically nonexisting positions. A dealer company can also create the illusion for the trader that the trader is present at the market and should find a way out of the situation and liquidate both opposite positions, whereas, in reality, they are nonexistent.

Many traders consider the possibility of keeping these opposite positions an advantage. This advantage allows them to hedge (or lock) their losing trades and to limit their losses in case the market moves against their initial position. At the same time, this possibility creates the illusion that loss of money is not final and that the money could be returned if the "right" way out of the situation was found. If you cannot stand the psychological stress of trading without such useless "placebo" methods, then it is better to reconsider further participation in this business.

WHAT ARE THE RISKS OF DOING BUSINESS WITH "BUCKET SHOPS"?

Legal issues (i.e., a set of acts governing and controlling the functions of banks, dealers, and broker companies in the FOREX market, established by government agencies) are of primary importance because traders have to entrust their money to the dealers. First, it is better for traders to make sure that their money is safe and that the breach of trust is impossible for the dealer.

I am not a lawyer, so I have no right to advise my clients on legal matters. The vast majority of dealer companies function in many countries, with various rules and regulations of which I am not aware. My recommendations are, therefore, based on my personal experience and preferences. In any case, you had better survey the problem yourself and preferably ask a lawyer for legal advice. The following sections outline my personal opinion concerning dealer choice, considering the security of capital invested in FOREX operations.

The Problem of Dealer and Broker Companies Abusing Client's Trust Exists on a Large Scale

Many countries lack any legislative jurisdiction governing dealer-customer relationships regarding the FOREX market, or government control over dealer and broker companies involved in speculative currency trading. That is the main cause of abuse of clients, especially when the client's money is used for market speculation and when unlawful extortion is charged.

The Majority of Broker Companies— Especially Small Ones—are Bucket Shops

Bucket shops are companies that do not have direct relations with the FOREX market, and do not execute real transactions on the real market. What they do is create an illusion of trading operations whereas, in reality, they only make mutual bets around rate changes between a client-trader and themselves. These bets are based on real current market quotas, but actually have nothing to do with the real market. If the client wins, the client gets paid from the broker company's own funds. If the client loses, the money remains in the broker's pocket.

In General, Operations of Bucket Shops Are Legal and Are Not Controlled by a Government

Many experienced traders know about practices of bucket shops but do not pay adequate attention to them. They think that the sources of gain or loss coverage are of no great importance. However, in reality, this belief leads to serious mistakes. When brokers try to maximize clients' losses, it aggravates contradictions between a client-trader and a company offering brokerage service. This can have very grave consequences for the client. Usually, such brokers do everything possible to make a client's operations on the money market difficult. They have at their disposal a wide variety of tools, ranging from various commission charges and other fees that the client is required to pay for the supposedly offered services, to quota manipulations that offer the client prices that are different from current market prices. There are some cases in which such companies have been liquidated, and their owners have disappeared with the clients' money. On the Internet, you can find numerous reports of clients deceived by such companies.

How to Determine If a Broker Company Is a Bucket Shop

You can determine with great accuracy if a broker company is a bucket shop by conducting these basic features of the company:

- The minimum necessary trading account size is less than $10,000.
- The initial margin is less than 2 to 4 percent or is not fixed at all.
- Positions are transferred to the next day not in accordance with the generally accepted rules based on the corresponding current LIBOR rates but with some other plan, and a trader is required to pay the interest charge at some fixed or floating rates.
- There are some extra charges in the form of commissions for each transaction and/or storage fees.
- Both opposite positions can be kept indefinitely (the so-called lock or hedge) for the same currency rate that is reflected in the client's statement.
- The setting of automatic stop and limit orders is governed by certain unreasonable restrictions, preventing order setting too close to the current market price if the fixed existing limit is exceeded, or by some other simulated restrictions on using automatically executed orders.

Bucket Shop Practices Are Widespread, Mainly among Dealer-Broker Companies in the United States, Eastern Europe, Southeast Asia, and Offshore Zones

Because bucket shop practices are so widespread, I would not recommend dealing with companies in the United States, Eastern Europe, Southeast Asia or offshore zones. It's better to be safe than sorry. I think the best area to open a trading account for FOREX operations is Western Europe, especially Great Britain. The reputable and easily checked European companies, or the European subsidiaries of reputable international banks, are the best choices to provide reliable service. Furthermore, Great Britain has a governmental agency—Securities and Futures Authority (SFA)—which overrules the dealer companies in the FOREX market as well.

Before Making a Final Decision, Remember to Check the Terms of Opening the Trading Account and Corresponding Transactions

The terms to consider, about opening a trading account and carrying out transactions, include: adding interest to the deposit, the opportunity to open a segregated account, the opportunity to trade under a bank guarantee, the time schedule for money transfers from one account to another, rules governing conflicts and settlements, and such. The right choice of a dealer greatly influences the results of your trading operations.

RECENT INDUSTRY DEVELOPMENTS

Some significant changes, both positive and negative, took place in the FOREX trading world over the past few years.

First let me mention three positive changes:

1. By the year 2006 the industry of FOREX trading had become more government regulated in the United States. Nowadays, the NFA regulates most of the dealers and introducing brokers conducting business in the United States, including foreign dealing companies providing services to U.S. customers. So, now the probability for a trader or an investor to become a fraud victim has greatly decreased.

2. Stronger competition among numerous dealing companies has made them offer their customers better services that include more sophisticated trading software, lower spreads, and faster and more accurate trade execution.

3. Reputable dealers now offer their customers the opportunity to trade contracts as small as $10,000. This is good for beginners, who today can make real trades without risking too much money while learning the business.

However, along with positive changes there also were two negative ones:

First, the same competition among dealers that improved quality of their services overall led to the situation that now almost every dealer could be considered a bucket shop. Today the dealers routinely trade against their customers, especially those individuals with smaller trading capital. In order to increase their revenues, some of the larger dealers on a daily basis carry an uncovered exposure totaling well over $100 million of the positions taken by their customers. At first glance it seems that there shouldn't be a problem. The rule of the game is that the house must always win and there are reasons to believe that most of the clients' trading capital sooner or later ends up in the dealer's pocket anyway, pretty much like in the gambling industry. (Dealers' back office statistics show that approximately 60 percent of their clients' total trading capital is being lost in trading annually.) However, unlike in the casino business where the house is always able to control each and every aspect of the game, there could be some very dramatic and fast changes in the market that wouldn't allow the dealer to cover its exposure before it becomes too late. Unexpected, almost instantaneous, and sizeable shifts in currency exchange quotes could be damaging to the point where a dealer would not be able to fulfill its financial obligations toward its customers.

The other change that I consider to be rather negative is the trend of most dealers lowering their margin requirements. Today it is quite possible to find a dealer offering to its customers a margin as low as 0.5 percent. Dealers present low-margin trading as an opportunity for customers to achieve greater profitability with smaller investment capital. It is true, but trading on full leverage also could easily cause the loss of the entire trading capital in a single trade in a matter of minutes. It looks like trading in the financial market is turning into a casino-style business, which is not good in my view.

PART II

Developing a
Trading Method

T he most difficult process is adjusting the human psychological factor, because in real life it is impossible to completely get rid of the psychological factor influencing human activity.

I think it is very important for the reader of this book to follow me in creating the method, beginning with the definition and identification of the problems that need to be solved. Then, after initial ideas are formed, we will continue to the development of effective trade principles and the creation of an integrated conception of systematic trading methods. I would like each trader to understand the essence and logic of my method, which allows a transition from vague emotions and desires to specific targets, in order to develop an effective trading technique. I think this approach to training is the best. It allows the trader to not only follow my line of thought but also, using the information acquired in this book, to extend each trader's individual (not only professional) experience, with the aim of critically evaluating the acquired information.

For this reason, I decided to violate the traditionally taught sequence of many books, manuals, and training aids, and state my book in the sequence of the development of my method. The first chapter (Chapter 4) in Part II is dedicated to trader psychology. The psychological problems shared by many traders will be addressed, and the conclusion will be proven that it is necessary to switch to a systematic trading method without forming a rigid mechanical trading system. This desire, and the necessity to get rid of the excessive and permanent psychological stress that negatively influences the results of my everyday trading, inspired me to develop the new systematic trading method I will present in this book.

In Chapter 5, the initial requirements for the optimal trade methods and the consequent trade systems are formulated. Next, some basic elements for the trade method development are described - using trading tools corresponding to the basic principles of effective trading. Along with my own ideas and elaboration, they will be used as the basic components of effective trading described in Chapter 7.

Each trader goes through mistakes, failures, and losses in his or her own way and in accordance with his or her personality and temper.

CHAPTER 4

Psychological Challenges of Speculative Trading

A successful trader's career mainly depends on his or her psychological stability in stressful situations, which are common in the process of trading. Theoretical knowledge can be acquired by reading professional literature; practical skills and experience are acquired in the process of actual trading. The most difficult process is adjusting psychological stress, because in real life it is impossible to completely eliminate the stress factor influencing human activity. Underestimating the stress factor could play a mean trick on traders and even completely block their abilities to make reasonable decisions in real trading situations. The psychological stress of those trading in the FOREX (and any other) market is extremely high. Traders must work under permanent psychological pressure, making decisions in highly unpredictable and uncertain market situations.

Each trader goes through mistakes, failures, and losses in his or her own way, in accordance with his or her personality and temper. Some might blame their failures on the market's "wrong behavior," which didn't comply with the trader's brilliant forecast and caused the failure of the magnificently planned speculative combination. Others blame themselves and their own inabilities to make right decisions in situations, which afterwards seem to be simple. It is an interesting fact that, in hindsight, traders usually find the decision that should have been made at the lost critical moment and can reasonably prove their point of view. Why can they find the right decision so easily and quickly in hindsight? Was the trader unable to do so at the right moment? I don't think it can be simply explained by looking at yesterday's situation from today's point of view. I do not think it can be explained by the fact that classical technical analysis allows for multiple explanations of almost any market situation. It is always possible to find an appropriate basic explanation for any market shift after the event takes place. In the heat of the moment, however, the trader was influenced by stress, and that stress caused the error. This is proven by the fact that most novice traders show exceptionally good (and even phenomenal) results trading dummy accounts but can't even come near those results when trading with real money.

Being permanently under stress, a trader can often make insufficiently considered, impulsive, and, therefore, wrong decisions that result in losses or premature liquidation of profitable positions, that is, in lost profit. Sometimes, after a few successive failures with various trades, traders becomes fearful of the market. They are in a state of psychological stupor, and even a simple market situation may cause panic. They cannot overcome their emotions or soberly evaluate the current situation, and they are unable to make any decision—reasonable or otherwise. In many cases when the market situation shifts against the trader's position, they can only passively watch the growth of their losses, because they are unable to make any decision at all. Often, after the market stabilizes and traders have the opportunity to calmly analyze daily diagrams of currency fluctuations, they come to the conclusion that the main cause of failure was not the lack of knowledge or training but their own emotions. However, the situation cannot be reversed. Time has passed, money has been lost, and everything should be begun again.

Another problem that causes severe and even catastrophic consequences is the trader's wishful thinking. In this case, traders are sure that their forecast of market trends is solely correct. They feel the market cannot and should not give any surprises. They do not consider other options that could be helpful or they think of other options in a vague and uncertain form. Sometimes, traders consider a market shift against their position as short-term and temporary. They begin to average their positions. They acquire new contracts at a lower price in the hope that the market situation will come back, and all the positions will become highly profitable. Afterwards, as the situation worsens, they will be able to come out of the market without serious losses. Being sure they are right, traders lose the ability to critically evaluate the condition of the market and accordingly their own position in the market. In this case, they consider only those basic and technical features that justify their wishful thinking, and they discard the contradicting features. This wishful thinking costs them dearly and can lead to psychological frustration. The market's "wrong behavior" not only deprives traders of a certain amount of money and often ruins their trading account, but also undermines their self-esteem and their hopes of being a winner in the trading battle.

After such a loss, traders blame themselves, repeatedly going through the details of the unsuccessful trade. They blame the market for the "wrong behavior" or themselves for errors in what then seems an absolutely clear situation. Sometimes, the trader-market relationship takes the form of a vendetta. Traders consider the market as their personal enemy, treat it in an unfriendly way (even with hate) and dream of immediate revenge. Doing so, they miss the fact that they are essentially blaming nature for changing sunny weather to rain. It is very important to be prepared beforehand for this change. Trades should always have close at hand one or a few options in case of sudden change of the situation/weather, so that their foresight assures their good time or good profit.

The third main psychological problem is trader uncertainty, especially when traders are inexperienced in abilities and skills—specifically about each market position they hold. Immediately after each position is opened and a money contract is bought, traders start questioning their choices. This is revealed most vividly in the case of a moderately active market at the moment of fluctuations close to the opening price of the position. Any movement (even insignificant) against their position causes traders to have an irresistible desire to sell the recently acquired contract to limit losses, until it is too late and the market does not shift too far away from their position opening price. On the other hand, an insignificant market shift in the desirable direction causes the same desire to eliminate the position, until it provides for any (even tiny) profit and before this profit does not turn into losses.

Scared and troubled traders rush and race about. They open and liquidate their positions too often, and experience many small losses and gains. Within a short period of time, they turn intermittently into bulls or bears. As a result, they suffer losses on a dealer's spread and/or commissions when there were no significant market changes, and all the market fluctuations were no more than just regular market "noise." Such losses are typical for beginners and individual traders with small investment capital or little experience and insufficient psychological preparation.

Not uncommon are cases of traders' impulsive decisions on trading, without any plans or serious preliminary market analysis. The position is opened under an impulsive, invalid emotional reaction. Often, it can be explained by traders' fears of losing a brilliant opportunity to earn money they think is being offered by the market at that moment. I have witnessed these attempts to jump onto the last carriage of a departing train, and such attempts have ruined a lot of traders. Many traders cannot calmly watch any kind of market movements. Some of my students have confirmed this reality. If they have no positions at the moment of more or less significant market movement, they consider it as a lost opportunity to gain profit. This can inflict a serious shock to them.

When they have no position, they seem unable to realize that each market movement can be considered both ways, and the opposite situation can quite possibly develop. Statistics show that, at each market movement, the chances to lose are much higher than to profit. How does it happen that reasonable people (who in everyday life, without any emotion, can watch a bank cashier counting other people's money) consider the fact of market movement as a threat to their own pockets? Why is other people's money in the hands of a bank cashier not considered as a lost profit, whereas capital shift on the market and the corresponding quote fluctuations are the causes of negative emotions? I think the answer is in the illusory simplicity of business itself, which is considered by many people as a good and simple opportunity to earn a lot of easy money. Similar notions are widely spread among novice currency traders. The soon traders abandon such ideas, the sooner they become professionally efficient traders.

The most difficult problem for every trader (regardless of their experiences) is to learn as quickly as possible how to recover quickly from losses, which are inevitable in this business. At the same time, they must learn to handle shocks and psychological damage inflicted by the losses, because these situations could negatively influence their future work.

The losses themselves and the fear of losing, both of which permanently torture traders, negatively influence their ability to make reasonable decisions in a complicated situation. These factors also undermine traders' ability to follow their own rules about trade strategies and systems.

I have become personally acquainted with hundreds of traders and have watched their activities. I have taught many students, and have had my own experience as a trader at various steps of my career in the currency market. Therefore, I have come to the conclusion that the main causes of trader failures in speculative operations in the FOREX market are without a doubt those associated with psychological trauma—the inability to control their own emotions and to find an adequate way to fight stress.

I have explored ways of solving the psychological problems that arise from operations in the FOREX market, with the focus on increasing self-resistance to stressful situations and increasing trade effectiveness. As a result of my research, I have managed to develop a trading method that also helps to withstand shocks and keep emotions under control. To solve the problem of stress, I had to separate the problem into several parts and solve them one by one.

First, it was necessary to develop the philosophical conception of my attitude toward market situations. By this I mean not only the general trade methods, which are discussed in the second part of the course, but also my own conception of the market and associated psychological problems, which most traders (including myself) have to overcome daily. The following formula is essential for my conception: I can't be wrong if I don't have an opinion.

I had this in mind as I thought about how to avoid unwanted stress and emotions that are associated with trading. When you find a way to make reasonable decisions not based on your own opinion about future market trends but in accordance with certain market signals, the problem of diminishing and almost completely eliminating psychological pressure and stress will be solved. The key issue in this case is a philosophical attitude about market trends—they are natural phenomena beyond human control and forecast.

The trick was to develop a secure and effective trade strategy that could advantageously use these natural phenomena. This formula seemed logical and could provide the basis for the development of a conceptual trading strategy. In reality, however, this job took considerable time. Nevertheless, the formula was used as a base for the development of my system-trade methods that I called the method of discrete-systematic trading.

Moving from the basic formula and general philosophical idea through intermediate conclusions, I came to the development of the trade method. This method provides for trading practically without emotions, and it became a very effective and profitable tool to earning money in currency speculations.

The logical chain of my arguments and intermediate conclusions is the following:

Idea 1. The main source of negative emotions and stresses is the unfulfilled trader's forecast, based on the trader's notion about market future trends.

Idea 2. To avoid unnecessary emotions and psychological pressure, it is better to completely abandon any notion about market future trends because this notion itself forms the forecast, which could be wrong.

Idea 3. The basic idea of the formula "I cannot be wrong if I don't have an opinion" transfers the moral obligation for trading results from the trader to the market. Now, the fluctuation of the market can be considered as a manifestation of the so-called "God's Will" or "Force of Nature," so the trader cannot be responsible for that.

Idea 4. It is possible to abandon attempts to make forecasts and still have a profit only if one stops trying to foresee market trends but follows them instead.

Idea 5. It is possible to follow market fluctuations using only the system-trade method and developing a trading strategy providing effective monitoring of these fluctuations.

Idea 6. One of the best methods of this approach could be the one providing the objective evaluation of the possibility of the market's movements at any moment in both possible directions.

Following this simple thought pattern, I was able to come to a final conclusion, which is shown in the box that follows.

Conclusion

The easiest way of solving psychological problems is to abandon attempts to trade on the basis of personal notion and forecast. Only the system trade, while making decisions automatically according to the preset plan, provides this opportunity. Turning to the system trade helps to solve the problem by decreasing psychological pressure on the trader and avoiding a lot of mistakes associated with psychological stress. The system trade itself not only helps traders to make operational decisions to increase profit; it also provides great psychological comfort necessary for the trader.

CHAPTER 5

Discretionary versus Mechanical Trading Systems

U tilizing a mechanical trading-system trade not only helps traders to make decisions and increase the profit, but also provides great psychological comfort for the trader.

There is nothing especially new in the conclusion of the previous chapter. The main idea is that I realized the necessity of switching to the system trade to try to lower the great psychological pressure I experienced when making every market transaction.

In reality, all traders use one or another system approaches to a trade; some of them use discrete methods whereas others prefer mechanical trade systems. However, the mechanical system lacks fundamental analysis elements, and the mechanical system's set of rules can easily be transformed into computer software. The system then can generate trading signals easy understandable by each trader having access to the system. The creator of such a mechanical system then becomes just a user of a system monitoring the computer-generated signals. The creative work ends after the system has been developed. In everyday life, the discrete trader can be compared to an artist (each time composing a new piece of art), whereas a system trader using a mechanical system is more like a craftsman (each time copying a masterpiece created by him- or herself or someone else).

Besides the many traders using their own trade systems, there are many actively developing market systems for sale as computer programs—the so-called gray and black boxes. Their prices vary widely, from a few hundred dollars to hundreds of thousands of dollars. Sometimes, these programs are developed for a certain corporation or bank. The only significant thing about any program is that the trader should be able to accomplish transactions in accordance with the signals generated by the computer software.

Considering the possibility of joining one or another group of traders, I had to analyze all the advantages and disadvantages of different approaches to trade. At first, I paid attention to the fact that the majority of successful individual traders I knew were using self-developed mechanical trade systems. The majority of unsuccessful individual traders use some sort of discrete trade method. Comparative analysis of the advantages and disadvantages of each approach gave me the ability to determine the causes of this situation. The comparative analysis also revealed the advantages and disadvantages of both approaches. You can conduct your own investigations, but I will share the conclusions that helped me make the decision to develop my own trading method.

The discrete method is known for the following two advantages:

1. Quick adaptability to market trend changes, which allows flexibility in choosing trade strategy and tactics corresponding to the current market condition;

2. Possibility to customize the same trading technique, considering the individual abilities of each trader such as size of his trading account and the time spent in trading operations.

The main, very serious disadvantage of the discrete approach is the unstable trade results due to the stress factors influencing the trader. In this case, the trader's mood and the state of his health are the primary importance and greatly influence the outcome of each trade.

Usually, a mechanical system used in trading almost completely eliminates the stress factor and reduces negative pressure on a trader, which is obviously a positive factor. However, it also prevents the trader from quick adjustment of trade tactics in the case of the market changing some of its characteristics. It doesn't allow flexible customization of the trading system in case other situations change, for example, change of the size of the trading account.

Because of these factors, I took a great interest in creating my own trading method that would contain the advantages of both different approaches, but would not have their disadvantages.

Before proceeding to this task, I had to formulate this task accurately. If the final goal is known precisely, then the way to reach it is much easier. That is why I began to build my method by formulating the requirements for it, which could be used as a basis for trading systems developed in accordance with my goals and tools available.

In my mind, there are eight main requirements to the ideal trading method:

1. It has to allow maximum adjustment to any trader's psychological character.
2. It should be universal, that is, effective and profitable regardless of a market trend at any given moment or period of time.
3. The system structure must be simple and consist of logical and understandable ready-to-use elements and units.
4. It has to generate specific price signals for the trader to open or close positions at the levels chosen some time in advance.
5. It must leave some room for a trader's creativity and allow the trader to choose certain tactical options in specific cases, so he would not consider himself to be a dependent tool in his own trading system.
6. It has to have some degree of flexibility to let a trader modernize and adjust the system in accordance with periodically changing market conditions, without violating the main principles and elements of the system's structure.
7. The system should also relieve a trader from extra emotional and psychological stress, and make his job comfortable and routine.
8. It has to include a customization feature so different traders, regardless of their experience, knowledge, training, size of trading account, and such could use the same method.

It would seem that these requirements for the trade method are excessive. The experience of many traders using the systematic trade in their operations shows that existing mechanical or other trading systems are often unable to satisfy the complete list of the listed requirements. For example, many systems that are satisfactory in trend situations become ineffective in a nontrending market. Change of market behavior could lead to negative results from a previously effective trade system, which obviously would then need replacement.

I am aware of many systems that are described by complex mathematical formulas, which are not completely understandable by a trader if the trader is not the author of the system. The common disadvantage of various (mainly mechanical) trade systems is the negative balance between profitable and unprofitable transactions. It is clear that the effectiveness of these systems can be maintained only in a case when the average profit of each transaction surpasses the average loss of each unprofitable trade.

Corrections in many well-known systems in the process of the trade are impossible. Therefore, the trader must accurately and unconditionally follow the initial demand enclosed into the system, without attempting to adjust it to the current market situation. The rejection of even a single element of the system leads to its complete ineffectiveness and failure.

The development of a single trade system satisfying all the aforementioned requirements and fitting any state of the market seems difficult or even impossible. I think the only way of satisfying these requirements is not the development of a single trade system. Rather, it is necessary to develop a diversified system trade method consisting of a set of system units that can be used as a basis for specific trade tactics at any given moment. It can be used according to a trader's free choice and considering the individual situation. Trade systems based on these principles should be complex and adjustable. These factors are necessary to optimize the systematic trading according to the current market situation and the trader's resources at any given moment. This optimization will provide the effective evaluation of market shift and trends at any given moment. The only thing to do is to find the tools for this probability evaluation with maximum accuracy and in minimum time. These ideas were then used as the starting point for further development.

In the process of preliminary analysis of existing trading systems, I paid attention to the fact that purely statistical dependencies in most of the systems are considered as secondary factors. In cases with a high volume of statistics, their true meaning is replaced by complicated mathematical calculations. I thought that if I managed to simplify and systematize methods of statistical probability evaluation, then it would be possible to develop the optimal trading technique combined with certain issues of technical and even fundamental analysis.

CHAPTER 6

Technical and Fundamental Analysis

I t would be unreasonable to try to invent something new without analyzing everything already invented in this field with proven effectiveness and value. Previous experience has always been the basis for further progress in any field of human activity, and trade is not the exception. This chapter describes the process of choosing components for the establishment of trading strategies and systems for the development of the discrete-systematic trading method using statistical dependencies.

The majority of traders who do not use system trade can be roughly divided into two groups: the first group includes the proponents of a mainly fundamental approach to market speculations; the second group includes traders making decisions based on technical analysis. There is a third (however not large) group of traders considering both approaches, but preferably using one of them. Disputes between the proponents of various approaches are typical for the Internet forums where professionals and amateurs meet to discuss urgent problems of the market. However, these forums look like the principal dispute described in *Gulliver's Travels*, where the Lilliputian governments quarreled about the right end on which to crack eggs.

I consider these disputes useless, and I am sure that the positive result itself is much more important than the means that helped to attain it. Both the fundamental and technical approaches in their classical form have their own advantages and disadvantages, which are mainly avoided or offset in the offered trading method. Let us begin with the problem facing the proponents of both trade conceptions. In this chapter, I describe some paradoxes that are in my opinion worth thinking about.

ADVANTAGES AND DISADVANTAGES OF FUNDAMENTAL ANALYSIS

Despite the fact that the market moves mainly due to fundamental factors, the problem of fundamental analysis is not simple. A fundamental trader needs to work hard to earn his bread. To carry out fundamental analysis effectively, a trader needs to have a deep understanding of macroeconomics, international finances, and political and social processes. He needs to adequately evaluate certain events and consider their influence on a specific currency rate, and he needs to forecast market trends in order to gain profit from the results of previous political or economic changes. The influence of each event or news should be estimated, considering all other factors affecting the market and a specific currency rate. However, even skilled economists, financial experts, political scientists, and professional market analysts are sometimes unable to complete this task. Also, the majority of small individual speculators often cannot evaluate the importance of a particular fundamental factor for the market.

In reality, market reaction to an obvious news event is often contradictory and unexpected. Chances of a correct forecast of market trends are inversely proportional to the number of traders sharing the same point of view. In other words, most traders are more often wrong than right in their understanding of fundamental events and phenomena, and their forecast of near-future market movements based on the fundamental data is erroneous.

These are five paradoxes that I noticed regarding the issue of predicting the market.

Paradox 1

The vast majority of FOREX traders are unable (because of their limited competence in macroeconomics and finances) to interpret correctly many of the various fundamental factors influencing the market, but the speculative trade based on fundamental analysis is widespread among individual traders-investors. Paradox 2 is interconnected with paradox 1.

Paradox 2

Despite the practical impossibility of forecasting market movements using fundamental analysis, there is a simple, rational, and fundamental explanation of previous market events and shifts after all.

It is relatively simple for the individual speculative trader who watches the main economic data and has access to sources of financial information, to predict the general trend of economic development of various countries. Hence, it is simple to compare economic growth rates of two separate countries or regions. This allows the trader to determine the main trends in changing national currency rates with greater probability. The disadvantage is the approximation used for the analysis, which is useless for short-term speculative operations because of the inaccurate determination of levels of entering and exiting the market. This leads to the next paradox.

Paradox 3

The vast majority of traders use long-term global economic trends. Being deliberate or forced proponents[1] of short-term speculations, they are unable to benefit from their own long-term forecasts and analyses.

A trader wants to know exactly why the various events and market movements occur, but this knowledge cannot help him much. I think the question Why? is of less importance to a trader, and cannot be compared to the importance of other questions that traders should answer before making their decisions. Questions like Where? When? and How many? should be of more importance for a trader—especially those who trade short-term positions or are involved in daily trading. In many cases, information about various market movements is not important. If the trader was late and did not take part in the previous movement, knowledge of the exact causes of the rate fluctuations does not help. Even if the profitable or unprofitable position was open at the moment of the market movement, the knowledge of the exact causes cannot help to reimburse losses or threaten the profit.

Sometimes, there could be certain exceptions to this rule, and these exceptions do not upset the generally secondary importance of the question Why? Exceptions include situations in which the long-term influence of news events on the market should be evaluated. Even in these rare cases, the trade operations based on the common sense method are possible and preferable.

Paradox 4

Many traders, whom I know personally, usually spend much time discovering and discussing the causes of previous fluctuations in the money

---

[1] I call forced proponents of daily and short-term speculation those traders who simply cannot afford long-term trade, despite their inclination to the positional trade. Their investment capital is not large enough to open and keep strategic positions. In the positional trade, stop orders should be fixed at a considerable distance from the initially opened position, and a single loss can completely ruin the trading account if it's a small one. Such traders often dream of multiplying the size of their trading account, so that they can switch into longer-term trading.

market. This knowledge has no practical value because by that time the train has gone and the market has already reacted to certain fundamental stimuli and the exchange rate is adjusted accordingly.

ADVANTAGES AND DISADVANTAGES OF TECHNICAL ANALYSIS

The proponents of technical analysis and technical trading methods are numerous—even though this science is relatively new. Their numbers grow every day, along with implantation of these revolutionary ideas into the arsenal of the vast majority of currency speculators. The founders of technical analysis (such as John Murphy) stated that technical analysis could become the only tool to forecast market movements and completely replace fundamental analysis. The number of publications on this subject has evolved, and now, even beginners can freely discuss head-and-shoulders formation. Technical analysis enjoys wide popularity among traders. Any computer software dealing with financial markets includes lots of indicators and other tools for technical analysis.

Technical indicators are used as the basis for the development of the majority of trade strategies and systems. Many traders skilled in mathematics try to optimize existing indicators and oscillators, as well as to develop new ones. The so-called black and gray boxes, which are, in essence, software with input trade algorithms, are based on these technical elements. However, not everything is so clear and unclouded in technical analysis. The main difficulty of technical analysis is an uncertainty that allows interpretation of almost each specific market situation in several different ways.

Besides, the basic elements of technical analysis widely used in everyday work do not behave the same way as they were described in textbooks and publications. See Figure 6.1. This way, the market prevents every trader (who has read the textbook and learned the scientific fundamentals) from profitable trading on the financial markets. Difficulties arise when technical analysis is used in daily short-term trading because of minor market fluctuations that, in essence, are just the market noise. This noise can be compared with radio interference hindering clear reception. Unfortunately, the amplitude of this interference is too high to be ignored in short-term trading, and it disturbs the market harmony. See Figure 6.2.

Paradox 5

The forecast on markets with a minimum number of technical traders among other participants is much easier. For example, daily plots of the DJIA, NASDAQ, and S&P indices often provide a technical picture that is

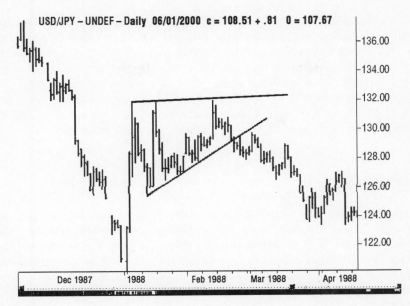

FIGURE 6.1 According to technical analysis textbooks, a triangle should be a reversal formation. As you can see on this picture, it's not always like that. So, to avoid being caught with the wrong opinion, the trade should rather be based on actual market behavior than on views, opinions, and projections.

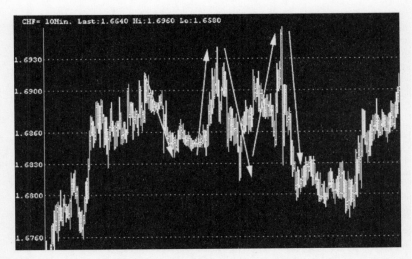

FIGURE 6.2 10-min USD/CHF chart shows how fast and volatile the market can be, sometimes making crazy swings in both directions. Despite all this craziness, the picture still makes perfect technical sense. Take a look at the formation. It is a broadening triangle we can clearly see on the chart.

close to ideal and easy to understand. However, stock-market traders traditionally prefer fundamental analysis, and the percentage of technical traders is still not sufficient. The FOREX market, filled with technically skilled speculators using the classic technical analysis tools, becomes more and more difficult to forecast.

Let us now look at the advantages and disadvantages of the main elements of classical technical analysis and select the most important elements, considering specific trade signals they send to traders.

PATTERNS

According to my observations, the probability of functioning of the most obvious formations like head and shoulders, double top, triangle, and such, has decreased greatly during the last three to five years. Today, the more obvious the formation is on the plot, the higher is the probability that the next neckline test will be false, and the main market shift will be in the direction opposite to the one indicated. See Figure 6.3.

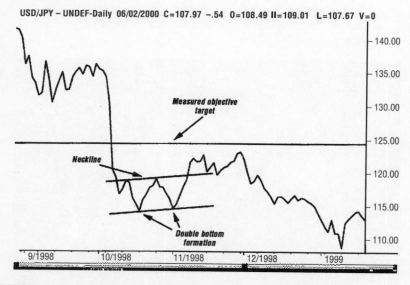

FIGURE 6.3 Slightly ascending but almost perfect double bottom formation on USD/JPY Daily chart. The measured objective target has not been reached, despite the fact that all the other attributes of a classic formation description are present. Even an unsuccessful attempt to come back and break the neckline from above is seen on the picture, but the run for the target has still failed.

The majority of traders I have met in my career do not have adequate knowledge of the technical analysis basics, and are unable to identify correctly certain classical formations or interpret widely known and practically used technical signals. However, the transaction level according to common practice should be expressed by the specific currency exchange rates, so we should pay adequate attention to them.

INDICATORS AND OSCILLATORS

Most indicators describe the market mainly in an ideal form, but reasonable thinking indicates it could not be otherwise, because such indicators are based on previous and current market information. The mathematical formulas, which determine the indicator lines and histograms, include the data for the previous period. Using them, a trader tries to make a forecast based on extrapolation. See Figure 6.4.

Unfortunately, in reality, the indicators that are good for the correct description of the past cannot provide a true picture of the future. I think the main drawback of these indicators lies in their plotting principle. This principle distorts the current market situation due to the artificial smoothing of

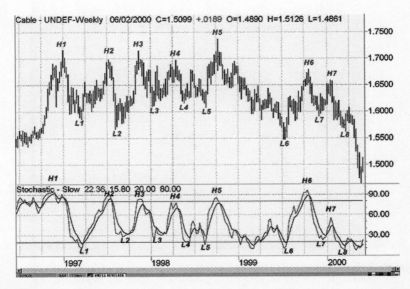

FIGURE 6.4 Cable on Weekly charts. Technical traders must love this picture. The indicator was able to provide the ideal description of the past. Unfortunately, it's too late now to benefit from it.

the real market signals by the mathematical manipulations on which an indicator formula is based. The momentum indicator signals are often too late, and the indicators intended to signal market overbought or oversold conditions are simply ridiculous. The market can move thousands of pips, even after the indicator gave the overbought or oversold signals on the daily or weekly graphs. See Figure 6.5.

It is not reasonable to keep floating losses of thousands of pips, expecting the market to return to your position levels, because it might never happen. The retracement could be shorter than the market's initial movement against the open position. In this case, the indicator can overpass the overbought or oversold zone before the market reaches the level of the initial position's opening price. Then the market renews its movement against an open position. Traders face this situation almost daily, but (having no better tools) they may consider this approach satisfactory for the development of various trading systems. See Figure 6.6.

Many traders simultaneously use several indicators in their trading systems. However, sometimes different indicators send contradicting signals. (See Figure 6.7.) Therefore, traders should select some of the indicators for certain situations and disregard the others. The selection of

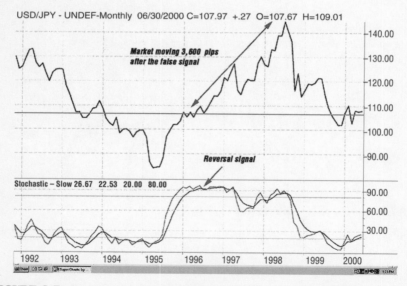

FIGURE 6.5 Technical traders should hate this picture, especially those who rely on such indicators in their trading. After entering an extremely overbought area, crossing toward the downside and sending a false sell signal, the indicator became practically useless. It took more than three years for the market to get back to the short position initial open price after going against it for 3.600 pips.

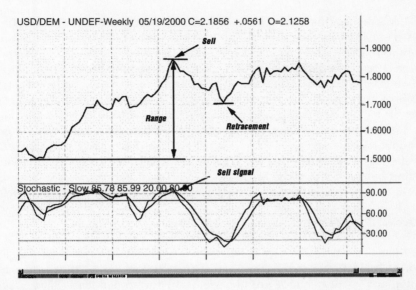

USD/DEM - UNDEF-Weekly 05/19/2000 C=2.1856 +.0561 O=2.1258

FIGURE 6.6 This shows a very nice trip for the indicator from the overbought area to the oversold zone. The market did not share its pessimistic view, though, and it refuses to follow the indicator down all the way.

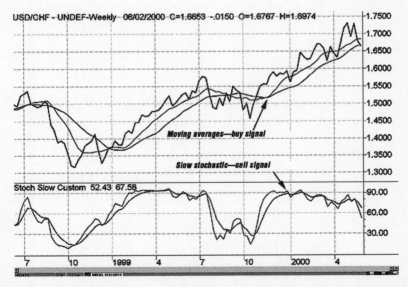

USD/CHF - UNDEF-Weekly 06/02/2000 C=1.6653 -.0150 O=1.6767 H=1.6974

FIGURE 6.7 Two different and the most popular indicators on USD/CHF weekly chart are sending controversial signals to traders. The picture needs some additional study and research for traders to make a decision. What if other indicators give the same controversial signals?

indicators requires strong skills and experience, but often the selection does not work in spite of those skills. Some traders often use different filters to exclude false signals, which complicates the system and make it even less effective. These trading systems (though not dependable enough) require more time for analysis and decision making. Many such trading systems often generate false signals, so the statistical ratio is in favor of the failed trades. It is clear that such a system can be profitable only if the average profit per one trade surpasses the average loss. Then, traders can be successful, not because of the dependable and effective system generating true trading signals, but mainly because of their money management skills and technique.

THEORIES OF TECHNICAL ANALYSIS

Technical analysis theories named after their authors (for example Fibonacci and Dow retracement theories, the Elliott Wave Theory, and the Gunn analytical method) are not useful for the trader. The Elliott Wave Theory sometimes describes market past events accurately, but gives only an approximate forecast of the future. I think the theory can be used only for mental exercises, but not as a real tool to earn money. It assumes a lot of options for a single case, and it relies on a trader's extensive experience

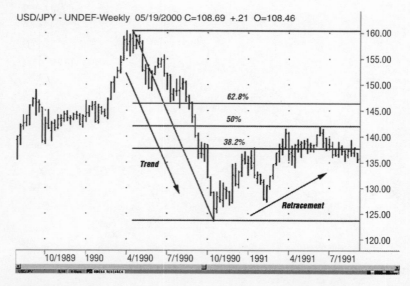

FIGURE 6.8   The trend was obvious, and so were the retracement and its target. For some reason still unknown to me, USD/JPY follows the Fibonacci ratios the most accurately, if you look back in history and compare other currency pairs.

in trading. However, this theory remains a puzzle toy for intellectual traders, rather than a practical tool for the majority of traders. Don't forget that Elliott himself was unable to use his theory in practice to make any money on the real market. (See Figure 6.8.) By contrast, the retracement theory can easily and naturally be used in my method because, in real cases, it provides precise numerical rate value levels. Traders can consider these values when they choose strategy and tactics, and they can plan their transactions for each trading period.

SUPPORT AND RESISTANCE THEORY

I think this theory is one of the best for the development of my trading method, because it is more precise than the retracement theory. Each buy or sell level at the moment of opening or liquidating positions is expressed in this theory by a certain value rate. This theory greatly simplifies calculations and provides an almost ideal profit/loss forecast. Furthermore, this theory is free from the disadvantages of practical trade methods and systems, which are based on a set of various indicators. There is no fluctuation smoothing effect, and there are no late trade signals. However, sometimes, as in the case of trading based on market formations, false signals are possible. See Figure 6.9.

FIGURE 6.9 The trend lines on the USD/DEM daily chart. Several triangle-like patterns are unmarked but are also clearly seen here.

CHARTS: POINT AND FIGURE, JAPANESE CANDLESTICKS

Both of these charts are designed, not for the real graphic reflection of the market, but for the analysis and forecast of future trends. There is no place for these charts in my common sense trading technique, not only because my technique needs no forecasting, but also because it was undesirable to complicate trading tactics that were effective enough without these extras. Also, I was too lazy to learn and memorize a lot of Japanese terms and designations, because the value of the method itself seemed doubtful to me. However, I recommend that my students get familiar with both types of basic charts and methods of using them, for the purpose of general knowledge and the ability to understand some professional discussions. See Figures 6.10 and 6.11.

As a result of an investigation, search, and analysis of the tools, trade methods and theories available to the trader, I came to the following conclusion: Some of these resources (especially if they do not require forecasting and provide exact market description) could be included in the method I was developing, but they could not solve the whole problem. In any case, I could not find a dependable combination of tools and theories

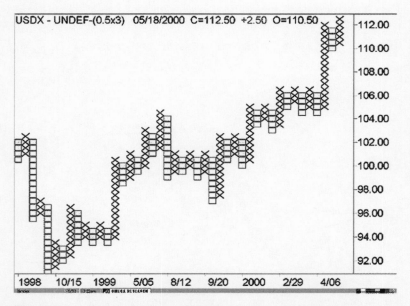

FIGURE 6.10 Point and figure chart sample. It seems pretty obvious when describing the past, but not so sure about the future. It has not been used in my trading method, but is is recommended for general education purposes only.

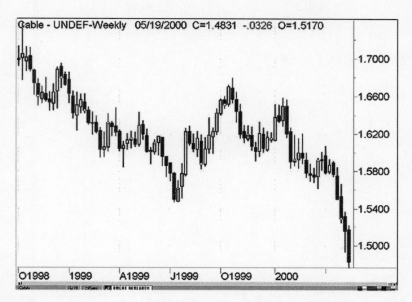

FIGURE 6.11 Japanese candlesticks chart sample. This is the oldest known study technique for market analysis, and it has also been popular in modern times. It is a perfect fortuneteller's tool, requiring a rich imagination and some knowledge of the Japanese language. There is no need for practical usage if you follow the common sense trading technique. The Japanese candlesticks chart sample is recommended for the purpose of general education, as well.

to develop the method that would satisfy my requirements. In the process of my practical work on the market, I noticed some repeated regularity in market trends that were not mentioned in the literature or used by the traders I knew. All these regularities were caused by similar extensions, and they clearly expressed statistical regularities in a certain sequence of market oscillations. I liked the idea of describing and formulating these regularities to use them in the method I was developing. This would take me close to the ideal successful trading method.

PART III

The Igrok Method

T he basic principle of the "Igrok Discrete-Systematic Method" (which I often call the common sense trading technique) can be stated briefly as follows: To speculate successfully on the FOREX market, traders should master a trading technique based on natural and statistically justified patterns of market behavior, to be able to effectively follow the market fluctuations without the necessity to foresee or forecast. The optimal solution could be a trading system based on natural market features and regularities.

Thus, I state that successful and consistent trading results can be achieved by investigating natural market features, and by using purely statistical estimation methods of market movement probability in any direction at a given moment. This probability estimation is based on the standard set of templates projected on the current currency chart. If a template coincides with the current market situation, I make the decision to enter the market. In every case, each trading position on the market is chosen in the most probable direction of the movement, which provides a positive statistical balance in favor of profitable trades. In this chapter, we discuss which features and regularities can be considered as natural market activities.

CHAPTER 7

Philosophy of the Igrok Method

It is known that the technical analysis philosophy is based on three main statements:

1. The market considers everything.
2. The market moves in accordance with trends.
3. History repeats itself.

Although I accept and share these statements, I offer my own philosophical conception on the basis of which I developed my trading method based on common sense. In general, it does not contradict technical analysis principles, rather it supplements them.

The following three main postulates are the philosophical basis of the new method and supplement the philosophical principles of technical analysis:

1. There are only two possible directions of a market movement.
2. The market moves permanently.
3. The market forms its trading range daily.

THERE ARE ONLY TWO POSSIBLE DIRECTIONS OF A MARKET MOVEMENT

Most traders do not fully realize this obvious statement. Somehow, it even contradicts the opinion widely held by traders that the side trend of market movement is a kind of third direction. However, on close examination, this side trend only occurs when there are alternating oscillations: up or down. The paradox is that the majority of traders cannot use that simple phenomenon to benefit from it. However, if you think about it, an acceptable trade strategy can be developed on the basis of this statement alone.

Some inferences from the first postulate turn out to be very important in benefiting from market rate fluctuations. Let us use common sense and elementary logic to formulate and then analyze some of these inferences according to their primary practical importance.

I consider the fact that there are only two possible directions of market movement very important because this limits the market options of reducing a trader's money. At any given moment, the trader has a minimum 50 percent statistical probability opening a new position in the right direction.

Here, I have to make a brief detour and somehow explain my position about a skeptic's opposite point of view about the same fact. Why should we consider the 50 percent probability of market movement in either direction as a negative factor, whereas the same probability about the trader is taken as positive? The reason for this seemingly contradiction is very simple. We consider the market behavior as primary and the trader reaction as secondary because, in making decisions and taking positions, the trader only responds to market changes.

So denying the assumption that trader activity causes market rate fluctuations, I suggest considering the market as spontaneously changing under the influence of factors unknown and unrecognized by us. Then, it can be concluded that a trader could survive in this environment only if he adjusts to these conditions. He should not try to dictate his will to the market, but only explore the ability to benefit from some of the market's features. One of these features is the market's ability to move in either of just two possible directions.

If this statement is taken as a starting point, one thing is clear. For a speculative trade on the FOREX or on any other market, it is necessary to know that the statistical probability of all trade results should exceed 50 percent to the trader's benefit in order for the final result to be positive. (This assumes the condition that the average profit per any successful trade exceeds the average loss per any unsuccessful trade). In fact, it would be reasonable to conclude that, to get generally positive statistical results, the initial probability of achieving success from any new position opened by the trader should exceed 50 percent. Positive statistical results need an effective evaluation method for this objective probability calculation at any given moment. For the development of such a probability evaluation system, the following statements (which are the basis of this method) are of primary importance.

A MARKET IS IN CONSTANT MOTION

This statement means that if a market is not moving in one direction, then it is moving in the opposite direction. In other words, a market's motionless state is practically impossible. Any position opened in any direction cannot keep the trader uninformed about the result for a long time; in a few minutes or hours it will generate either an essential profit or an essential loss.

An essential profit now and later means a profit equal to or exceeding 25 percent of each trade's trading capital (or initial margin). For the major currency rates at an initial margin of 2 percent, it equals $500 for any minimal standard contract of $100,000.

Because of specifics of money market trends, substantial fluctuation amplitude of each trend is a rule, whereas a narrow and more or less continuous side trend is rather rare. Any taken position may generate profit or loss in a few days, which will be several times more than the initial margin size. This particular feature of the money market allows everybody to conduct a very interesting experiment/investigation. First, you should picture two parallel lines at a distance of 50 to 70 or even 100 pips from each other, drawn on a randomly chosen area of a chart showing the prehistory of any of the major currency rates (distinguished by their almost ideal liquidity and highest activity). Then, imagine that every time the market crosses this line in the upward direction, we open a long position. Then, imagine that every time the market crosses this line in its downward direction, we open our short position. In other words, the open short position is always below the lower line, and the open long position is always above the upper line. See what happens next. This simple experiment helps to explain that, regardless of the initially opened position, this action will immediately bring a substantial, progressing profit. In another scenario, closed with a loss and being reversed in the opposite direction, the new position would sooner or later generate the same profit; or, as a minimum, would cover the initial losses by the subsequent profit. In this case, the multiple market movements up and down crossing the drawn horizontal lines on the charts will cover the initial loss or any possible series of consecutive losses. This is true even if the zone we use is optional and we choose it in the very middle of any real horizontal trend seen in the past—even the most prolonged in the trading history of any major currency pair. See Figure 7.1.

There is a logical conclusion based on this simple experiment/investigation: Any random position opened at any randomly chosen price will allow the trader either to get a substantial profit immediately or to be in a break-even situation after a relatively short series of simple, automatically performed transactions.

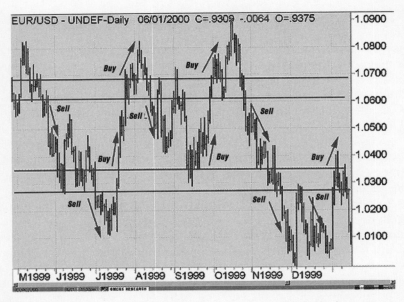

FIGURE 7.1 Two randomly chosen 70-pip ranges on EUR/USD chart. As you can see here, any long position taken at the upper lines of each range or short position open at the lower line of both ranges sooner or later becomes profitable. This is true even if the choice to open a position was made based on a coin toss. After several possible losses and reversals, at least a break even is practically guaranteed. Try this for your own home research on any charts of major currency pairs.

In the foregoing discussion, I somehow simplified the situation by not considering the probability of draining the trading account because of so many turnovers. I have no intention of suggesting this probability as an option to the readers, but only to use it as a theoretical illustration of the statement of a market's permanent movement. Opportunities to use the statement in practice will be described in the following chapters of the book.

Now it is time to discuss the third and final basic philosophical postulate of my method.

THE MARKET FORMS ITS TRADING RANGE DAILY

The third postulate is as logical and natural for the market as both previous postulates, and it is very important to a trader. It states that, during one trading day (i.e., 24 hours), the market should start and finish a certain trading range. This range can be simply calculated based on an analysis of each currency rate's behavior on the preceding day even for a relatively short period. In other words, for any currency rate, there is the so-called daily operational task to fluctuate with amplitude of a certain value. This minimum to average fluctuation amplitude is not the same for different currency pairs. Also, from time to time, it deviates for the same currency pair, depending upon market activity due to cyclic oscillations. Nevertheless, the intraday fluctuations mean amplitude is more or less stable for each cycle. The duration of each cycle is measured in months, optimally providing the base for the approximate calculations of the minimum to average fluctuation amplitude. This calculation allows a trader to conduct an approximate advance forecast for the current day.

The practical use of the three basic postulates of the method will be discussed in subsequent parts and chapters of this book.

After creation of a philosophical basis of the method, formulating the basics strategy and tactics of a speculative trade was an easy job for me. It involves six steps:

1. The fundamental nature of the exchange rates' fluctuations is not denied by the method, but in practice it is not taken into consideration because it does not directly affect the trader's one and only goal, which is to gain speculative profit on the basis of these fluctuations.

2. The basis of the method is the trader's reaction to trading signals generated by the market itself. The application of substitute and artificial derivatives such as indicators, oscillators, and other man-made instruments is essentially limited in this method. (In reality, for the market analysis, I use only two or three indicators, which have no independent significance and serve only to confirm basic signals in accordance with the principles of my trade methods.)

3. The signal's identification on a buy and sell is based on a set of market behavioral models. The trade takes place when one of the trading templates corresponds with a current market situation.

4. The templates represent a set of standard variants of a trader's actions executed in a certain sequence.

5. The basis of all templates used in the method is the estimation of a market movement probability in one or the other direction. The estimation of probability is made with the use of some rules of technical analysis combined with money management elements in each of the templates.

6. Sometimes there is a possibility of using several different templates in the same specific market situation. In this case, a final choice depends on the trader's will, his individual desire to undertake an increased risk in exchange for an opportunity to gain an essential profit.

It is clear that the trader's basic task is to be on the right side of the market at the right moment. Basically, it is supposed to be his only concern.

My trade method is based on probability evaluation of the market future behavior, which, as stated earlier, represents a set of templates that are formulated in advance and then tested. The trade does not occur until one of the templates corresponds with a current market situation. If and when a template corresponds with the real market situation, the decision to open or to liquidate a position will be taken by trader almost automatically. In addition to some elements taken from technical analysis, I also apply some issues concerning money management. They are an important part of a trade strategy and serve as the additional insurance in the event that the signal subsequently appears false and the market changes its direction.

Therefore, it is possible to tell that different templates represent combinations of trade signals received on the basis of the technical analysis, estimation of probability of common statistical laws, and money management.

CHAPTER 8

Evaluating Probabilities Using Technical Analysis

The probability evaluation technique is based on common market laws and is conducted in accordance with technical analysis rules.

It is clear that, at any given moment, the probability of the market moving in one direction or the other in the future is unequal. Also unequal is the probability of a possible profit or loss receipts on any position taken. This probability depends on many factors: time of day, sequence and amplitude of the previous fluctuations, long-term and short-term trend directions, current technical picture, direction and speed of market's movement at the present moment, and other factors. The various combinations of these factors can be identified, classified, and serve as the base for constructing standard models of the market behavior.

After this preliminary research is done, selecting effective tactics for each concrete trade should not be too complicated. If you know and are able to identify these laws, objective probability evaluation will replace the necessity of having your own opinion about future market behavior. Therefore, each new position taken by a trader in the market, from the moment of its opening, has to have a considerably high probability to become profitable rather than unprofitable.

For an initial and rough estimation of a direction probability of the next market movement, I mostly use technical analysis with the exception of those elements that I consider insignificant or insufficiently accurate. In particular, I do not use any indicators with the exception of MACD and RSI; the only purpose of their use is to identify divergences on daily, weekly and monthly charts. See Figures 8.1 through 8.4.

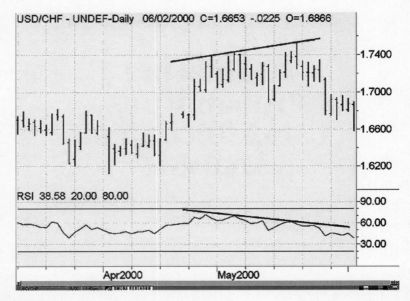

FIGURE 8.1 USD/CHF Daily chart picture. It is a sample of bearish divergence on the RSI indicator.

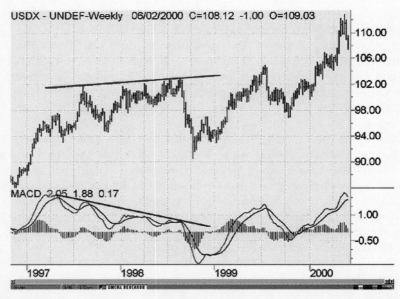

FIGURE 8.2 This is another bearish divergence. This time, it is shown on the MACD indicator on the USDX weekly chart. As you can see, it worked exactly as it was supposed to, despite the fact that the major trend is up.

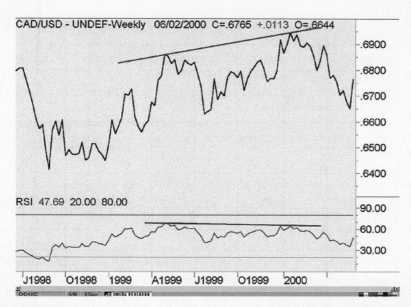

FIGURE 8.3 One more chart and one more bearish divergence against the trend. The correction, though, wasn't big enough to reach the bottom of the previous dip.

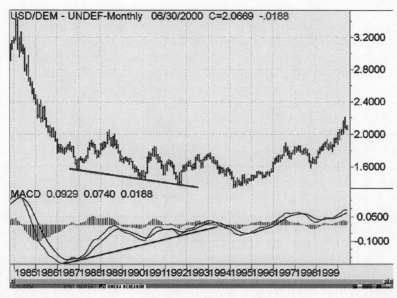

FIGURE 8.4 Here is an extremely important and interesting picture. A bullish triple divergence seen on the monthly USD/DEM chart and the MACD indicator gives a very strong signal in favor of a major trend reversal after the downtrend, which lasted for many years from its 1984 acme to its end. This divergence probably indicates the final turn into a major USD uptrend against all European currencies.

61

Besides technical analysis, I also use simplified statistical analysis made on the basis of long observation of the market behavior and study of its common laws. Many laws can be quite well explained from the common sense point of view, as well.

Such preliminary probability evaluation allows me to avoid the most common mistakes at opening and liquidating of my positions. The criteria follow.

- Usually, the probability that the market will continue its current movement in the present direction is higher than the probability that the market will soon change direction to the opposite.

Because the market has a high degree of momentum, the logical conclusion would be that opening a position in a current prevailing direction already gives a trader some statistical advantage of making a profit, rather than having a loss in such a case. However, even though it directly follows from one of the basic postulates of the technical analysis (the market moves in trends), many traders prefer to search for the opportunity to catch the moment of the market transition from one direction to another, instead of going with the trend. My own observation shows that many novices intuitively feel this law and open the majority of their positions (in the very beginning of their trading careers) in a direction of a current market move. In fact, the less theoretical knowledge and practical experience a beginner has, the more expressed such a tendency is. Although they don't yet feel capable of predicting future changes in the market behavior and don't try to do so, they base their trading on what they see on the screen.

Because the FOREX market has a very high volatility, often such a tactic is justified and brings novice traders success during the initial period of their trading careers. This is why the overwhelming majority of the novices succeed while practicing dummy trading or even trading with real capital in the beginning. Unfortunately, this ability to go with the market soon disappears. Then it becomes substituted with analysis, mostly in accordance with knowledge received from books. Instead of simply following market fluctuations, traders begin to predict its future behavior and try to act in advance. From that point on, the majority of new positions are based on analysis and forecasts, and very often against the current market movement. From the moment strategy is shifted to mostly picking tops and bottoms, the chances to survive in business are sharply lowered.

From my point of view, the formula "sell on weakness, buy on strength" has an obvious advantage over another popular formula "buy low, sell high." The latter better fits a longer-term trader or investor rather than a short-term speculative trader, whose basic purpose is to enter and exit the market fast enough to get a relatively modest profit and then to secure it. In real trading conditions and especially in a day trade, it is much more difficult to define a point or even an approximate zone of a market turn, than to receive fast profit, catching the market on the run and opening a position in a direction of its current movement. Therefore, any trade tactics providing a position opening in a direction of movement (that already has begun) can be considered preferable in comparison with tactics focused on picking extreme market levels (tops or bottoms) to open a position against the prevailing direction at the moment.

- If the market had committed a significant move in some direction during the day, there would be a high probability of some extension in the same direction during the next day. The same assumption can also be used for analysis of weekly and monthly charts. See Figures 8.5 and 8.6.

The trend is one of the main market's features and occurs frequently. There is nothing unusual in this fact, and the FOREX market is famous for

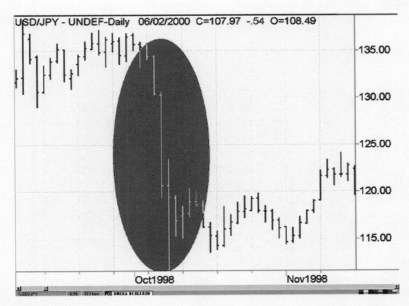

FIGURE 8.5 This is a very impressive sample of my statement: A strong and volatile move in one direction, with the closing price of the day almost at the very bottom of its range, continued during the next day. Despite the fact that the volatility of the third day was big, the closing price was closer to the top of the day than to the bottom, and therefore, no further extension is seen.

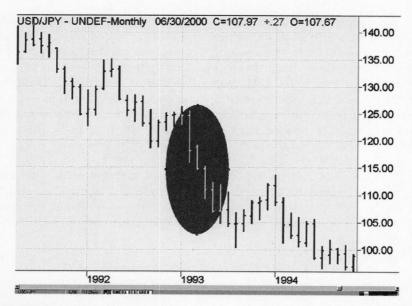

FIGURE 8.6   This picture illustrates the same assumption as that in Figure 8.5, but in a bigger time frame.

its trends. Simply looking at the charts you can relatively easily identify the day, week, or month when a movement has begun. Such a period is characterized by the prevalent tendency in one or another direction and by an essential difference between the opening and closing prices of each bar on the charts. See Figure 8.7.

While conducting simple statistical analysis of daily and weekly charts at the end of each trading day and week, pay attention to the closing price of this day or week. If the market closed near the high of the last bar, there is a great probability, that the high of the following bar will be even higher. See Figure 8.8.

If the market closing price was almost on the low of the bar, then most likely that low of the following bar will be even lower. See Figure 8.9. Because gaps on the FOREX market's daily and weekly charts are very rare, the open price almost never coincides with the future high or low of the bar.

For example, if the day's closing price was near the high, on the next day the probability of a repeated attempt to reach and exceed the previous day's high would be much greater than the downward market movement. In other words, the market usually trades in both directions from

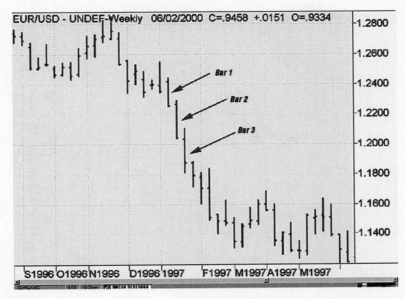

FIGURE 8.7 An acceleration of a downtrend on the EUR/USD weekly chart indicated by a significant difference between open and close prices of each consecutive bar.

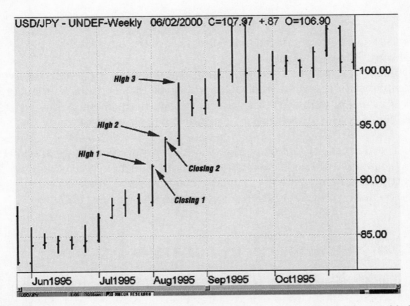

FIGURE 8.8 Typical uptrend sample. Each closing near the top of the weekly bar with an above-average range statistically leads to a continuation of the move in the same direction.

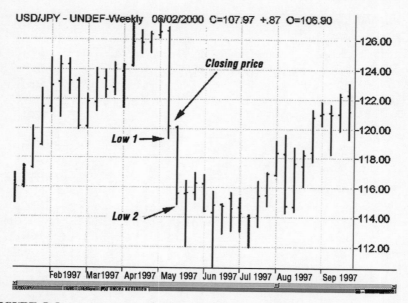

FIGURE 8.9 In the case of a downtrend or fast and deep correction, each closing near the bottom of the weekly bar with an above-average range leads to a continuation of the move in the same direction.

the day's open price, but the main direction of the day is mostly the same as during the previous day.

It is also important to keep in mind that if a trend is present, the average number of consecutive days on which the closing price of the day is lower or higher than the opening price is four. In my memory, the highest number of consecutive positive or negative day closings was nine.

- The purpose of technical analysis is not to predict where and when the market will go, as many traders think. The main goal of analysis is to define in advance the critical points or levels. Then, based on this research, you can build a trading strategy for the next trade.

END-OF-THE-WEEK AND END-OF-THE-DAY ANALYSIS

Creating and improving my trade method, I have developed a routine procedure of market analysis. The research is made regularly and always precedes any real actions on the market. This procedure provides me with the preliminary analysis of a current market condition at the end of each trading day. It begins with definition of key points, critical zones, supports and resistances, and also includes preliminary and rather rough probability evaluation of the main market direction during the next day. At the end of each week, I do such analysis for the whole next week, too. Despite the fact that this part of the chapter is large in volume and contains many steps that a trader needs to take before he completes his daily routine analysis, the actual time you will spend on the daily procedure is unlikely to exceed 15 to 20 minutes.

The Weekly Chart Analysis

Preliminary analysis on weekly charts is conducted at the end of the week, and is supposed to be updated at the end of each trading day.

(The fact that you prefer a short-term trade is not so important. Longer-term market analysis should be done even if you consider yourself as a day trader and the majority of your positions are taken and liquidated within the same trading day. To make a right decision on an intraday trade, you also have to see the bigger picture, to identify key levels and current longer-term trends. As a matter of fact, dividing the FOREX market participants among short-term, intermediate-term and long-term traders seems a bit artificial to me. For example, I personally never refuse to keep my position open for a longer period of time if there is a strong reason to believe that the current trend will continue. Transforming an intraday trade into a positional trade, revising my initial plan and changing the time frame can do the necessary adjustment.)

The purpose of this analysis is to define the prevalent intermediate- to longer-term trends and identify on the chart critical points, zones, and levels. Those levels should be located relatively close to the previous week's closing price and within the reach of a potential next week's range. All technical formations and patterns have to be taken into consideration and identified as well. The trendlines should be drawn and the measured objective targets (if any) calculated. The charts, along with the lines drawn on them, should be saved in your computer and updated every day.

(The Omega SuperCharts (end-of-day) software, which I use for intermediate and long-term analysis, is the best software I know. This computer program allows you to save in the memory a large number of graphic windows with lines drawn on them and, if it is necessary, any number of indicators.)

Every day, in accordance with the market's changes, you should plot a new day bar and revise the lines that have been drawn on the weekly chart the week before. If necessary, remove the old lines and add new ones. For example, even for a day trader all the trendlines, support, and resistance lines lying within 2 to 3 days of an average trading range could be important. Those critical points that are on a distance up to 300 to 500 pips in both directions from the closing price of the day have to be noted and placed on the chart. The levels nearest to a closing price are the most important and require more attention. You have to precisely calculate the critical point where this level might be penetrated by the market in the nearest future.

The most basic task, but at the same time the simplest, is to define a direction of a current intermediate-term trend. I don't think anybody has a problem with this definition, because presence or absence of a trend is usually visible from the first look at the chart. Therefore, I want only to remind you that analysis should be conducted on both bar charts and line-on-close charts.

- You should begin with the search of already formed technical formations (head and shoulders, double (triple) tops/bottoms, triangles, wedges, flags, channels, etc.). They should be identified in the following order:
  - **a.** complete formations, with already broken trend/or necklines (critical lines)
  - **b.** complete formations, but the critical levels have not been broken yet
  - **c.** formations, coming nearer to completion
  - **d.** formations that are just starting their development

  (In the case of d, we are making some projections for the future. This is the most complicated task, and requires certain practical experience and some imagination from a trader.) After identification of a technical formation, you should draw and save all necessary lines forming this pattern, including the possible measured objective target, if this given formation allows defining it. See Figure 8.10.
- Drawing trend lines and horizontal supports and resistances will be the next step. Identification and allocation on the chart of possible horizontal and inclined channels limited by two trend lines is also very important. Such lines should be drawn only according to certain strict rules. According to the laws of geometry, it's possible to draw a direct line through any two points in space. Therefore, trend lines, only if they are not necklines of one of the technical formations, will make sense only when they are drawn through a minimum of three important points on the analyzed chart.
- The trend lines should be drawn through three consecutive tops, or three consecutive bottoms, or highs and lows of daily and weekly bars. Preferably, the bars should not intersect the trend line along the way. The line, which has many casual and unconfirmed intersections, is less reliable for a trader. A perfect trend line should be placed on a

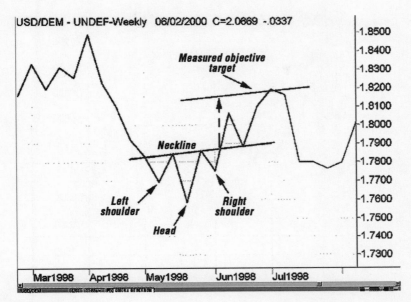

FIGURE 8.10 This is a very rare, really technical picture. This is an ideal inverted head and shoulders formation illustrating any classic textbook description of its appearance and the sequence of its moves. All the necessary elements are present. After breaking the neckline and sizeable follow-through, there was a perfect correction, which attempted to break the neckline once again but from the opposite side. Then, a measured objective target was reached.

chart, without being intersected, but only being touched on one side. A trend line that was already infringed in the past, even once, cannot be considered as reliable, and you should build trade plans on its basis with sufficient care. See Figures 8.11 and 8.12.

- Drawing of Fibonacci lines should become the third step, which should be drawn on two kinds of charts: open-high-low-close (OHLC) (bar chart) and line-on-close chart (line chart). These lines should be saved on the charts and regularly revised and clarified according to changes in the market. Fortunately, modern charting and analytical computer programs simplify the process considerably. See Figures 8.13 and 8.14.
- Checking some indicators finishes the analysis of weekly charts. My method assumes very limited use of such tools. From all varieties of indicators, I use only RSI, MACD, and very rarely, slow stochastic. These three indicators serve me as auxiliary only and serve only two purposes: to receive the early warning of a possible turn of the market, by receiving a divergence signal between the fluctuation chart and listed indicators; or to confirm the change of a trend.

FIGURE 8.11 After numerous false breaks, the trend doesn't make sense any more and cannot be used as a trading signal—even if (as in this case) the trend has eventually continued.

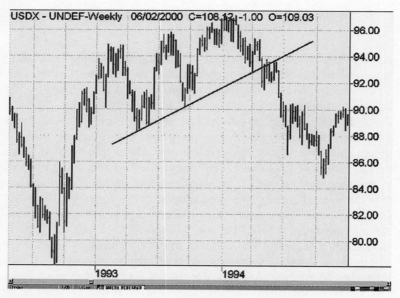

FIGURE 8.12 On the break of a trendline like the one shown on this chart, a short position should be established.

FIGURE 8.13 Fibonacci retracement lines drawn on the USD/CHF daily bar chart.

FIGURE 8.14 Fibonacci retracement measuring tool applied to the line-on-close chart.

Analysis of daily charts is similar to analysis of weekly charts. The difference between them is basically that a smaller time interval allows you to define critical levels and zones more precisely and accurately, to plan a future trade. Furthermore, some formations that cannot be identified on the more large-scale charts, can be visible on the charts with the shorter time frame. In addition to the points just listed, you should conduct the search of gaps on daily and weekly charts.

The FOREX market is densely filled with technical traders and, for this reason, the formations frequently do not fulfill their destination to give traders reliable signals to enter a market and make some projection for the future.

Gaps on Daily Charts

Because the FOREX market works five days a week around the clock (in contrast to other financial markets), we don't see classical gaps the way they appear on future and stock markets. As is generally known, a gap is a break between two consecutive bars on the chart, when the low of the previous bar is above the high of the previous one or the high of the previous bar does not reach the low of the bar directly following it. Such gaps, in their classic description, are very rare on the spot currency market. Nevertheless, breaks on exchange rates charts exist, though they look a little different than they are described in technical analysis books.

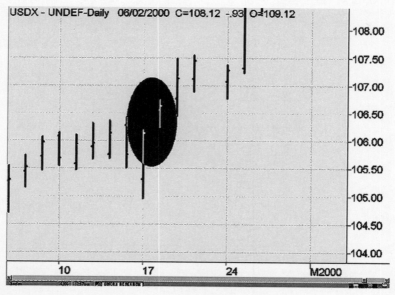

FIGURE 8.15 An unfilled gap on the USDX daily chart.

Gaps (or formations I define as gaps) with reference to the FOREX market are formed more often between Friday and the following Monday, and are very rare in the middle of a week. They look like breaks between the closing price of the previous day (and accordingly the previous week, if this day is Friday) and the low or the high of the following trading day (occasionally also all of the following week). The examples of such gaps are shown on a formation like the one in Figure 8.15.

Most of the time, the market comes back to the gaps a bit later and completely covers the price break formed on the chart. The gap identification is very important but usually I don't trade on return and closing of such a gap. Formed some time back, a gap gives me additional confidence if my position is open toward a gap, and provides a warning signal if the position has been opened in the opposite direction.

Combs on Daily Charts

A formation such as a comb doesn't exist in technical analysis. This is my own definition of the specific formation, which sometimes appears on daily bar charts. (It is also common on intraday charts.) A comb represents a specific kind of trend. The specific feature of a comb is that you can draw a trendline on a certain part through highs or lows of any three of five consecutive daily bars. The trendline will make sense if it's directed

FIGURE 8.16 Combs on USD/DEM daily chart.

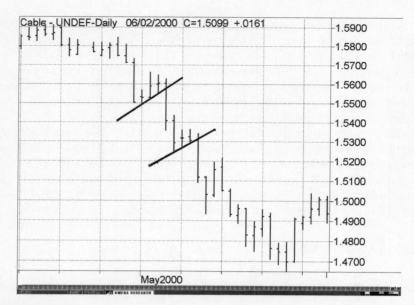

FIGURE 8.17 Medium-term local trends on the USD/DEM daily chart. I called these kinds of patterns Combs.

under some angle upward, drawing through lows, and angled down, drawing through highs. The examples of such formations are shown on the formations in Figures 8.16 and 8.17. A comb is one of my favorite patterns, which gives a reliable signal to enter the market with the appropriate position in the moment of a trendline intersection.

OTHER FORMATIONS ON DAILY AND WEEKLY CHARTS

Identification of various formations on the intermediate and long-term charts should be conducted in accordance with technical analysis rules. Identification includes head and shoulders, double (triple) top (bottom), rectangle, triangles, wedge, flag, diamond, and so on. Usually, if you have basic knowledge and some experience, it shouldn't be a problem to identify them. However, I repeatedly found myself in situations in which even relatively experienced traders were unable to identify formations that were quite obvious from my point of view. Sometimes they saw such patterns in places where I, having sufficient imagination and significant practical experience, was unable to identify them as such—with all my diligence and even with the help of another trader.

Different interpretations of technical patterns and formations are frequent among traders. Their interpretations of possible market behavior based on such identification also differ. As I already mentioned, the FOREX market is densely filled with technical traders, and for this reason formations frequently do not fulfill their destination to give a trader a reliable signal to enter a market and make some projection for the future. According to this fact, a trade on a projected target frequently can be unsuccessful. However, we shouldn't ignore these formations also. We will discuss how to use these formations and how to ensure that we are safe in the chapter devoted to trading signals.

CHAPTER 9

Basic Trading Strategies and Techniques

Trading signals that I use in my method are not much different from support and resistance theory and chart formations taught in books on classical technical analysis. In such books, none of the crossings, divergences, or other signals that I use with various indicators is accepted at all. My own interpretation of these signals is different from the classical and standard, so each of them requires a separate and detailed explanation.

TRADING BASED ON ASCENDING AND DESCENDING TRENDLINES

Ascending or descending trendlines practically always give a perfect opportunity to construct a trade plan based on them. The clearer, more distinct, and more obvious a trendline is, the easier the trade should be. I recommend that you pay attention to the phenomenon I have discovered, which for some reason has been overlooked in numerous technical analysis handbooks and recommendations:

Any trendline correctly drawn through three or more points will be broken sooner or later. If such a line hasn't been broken yet, it becomes a zone of attraction for the market to return to it.

There is an obvious and rather simple explanation to this fact. Significant stops accumulate gradually behind such a line and the market then begins to successfully pursue on them.

The probability of a false break is higher if such a line has had only a few contact points for a long period of time, and the market hasn't done significant retracement along the trend yet. See Figure 9.1

In other words, a sharp and impulsively high amplitude movement followed by the break of a trend line, should serve as a warning that the break may be a false one. By contrast, the long period of market consolidation directly before the break more often specifies the high probability that significant follow-through or trend change will follow the break.

In any case, even if you don't know whether the trend line will be broken now or later, or whether this break will be real or false, the next approach to the trend line gives an opportunity to open a new position. At first you trade away from the trend line. As the market emerges from underneath the line, open a sell position. If the market emerges from the top, it gives you a signal to open a buy position. Stops, as always, are obligatory and they should be established directly behind the line, at a distance not exceeding 10 to 15 pips from it. Simultaneously, with the stops liquidating your initial position, you may place so-called entry stops for opening a new position in an opposite direction. For example, the line is used as a support or resistance (depending on the specific sit-

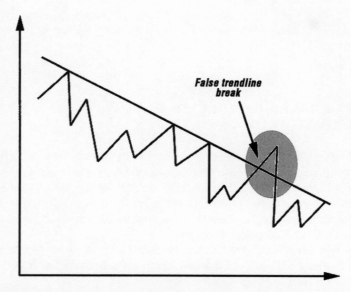

FIGURE 9.1   A false break of the trendline is usually a confirmation of the ongoing trend continuation.

uation) and as a border. When the market crosses this border, it automatically gives a signal to change direction of a trader's position. See Figure 9.2.

There are three possible subsequent scenarios:

The First Scenario
(No Break of a Trendline Occurred)

If the trendline does not break, then according to the first two basic postulates of the philosophical conception, your initial position will be to open away from the trendline, which will bring some profit in a short period of time. After placing stops, you can relax and enjoy watching a profit growing and accumulating on your position. Take profit later according to the trade plan made in advance within the time frame you selected. See Figure 9.3.

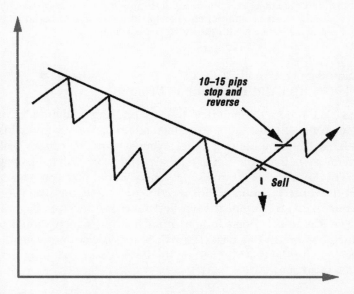

FIGURE 9.2 A trendline is like a borderline between the market territory and open space. Right ahead of an ascending trendline, you should take a short position. Be cautious, because every line drawn through any three significant points will be broken sooner or later. Each subsequent market approach to such a line increases the probability of a break. If a break takes place, stop and reverse your position a short distance from the break point.

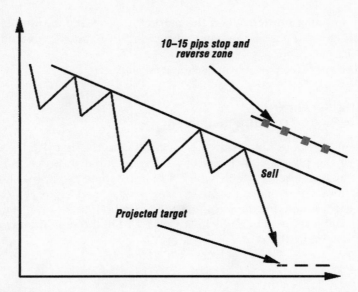

FIGURE 9.3 This scenario is the most desirable for a trader. A trendline held once again, and a short position open ahead of the line should be liquidated and profit realized in accordance with the initial trading plan.

The Second Scenario
(Good Move after the Trendline is Broken)

This one is a bit more difficult than the first one, but it shouldn't cause exceptional problems for traders. After light stress caused by initial loss, you soon will experience emotional relief. When a trendline breaks, following an active move in the direction of a break, your stops will be activated automatically. After losing 20 to 30 pips on an initial position, you already have another open position in the direction of a trend, on which you gradually accumulate profit when the market moves farther from the point of a break. See Figure 9.4. Don't forget to place stops, which should protect your new position. In this case, the risk of losses on a new position will again be equal to the risk you had on the initial one. Next, pray the break wasn't the false one.

The Third Scenario
(The Trendline Break Was False)

The third scenario is the most unpleasant one for a trader. Prayers don't help when a false break occurs. After the break, which activates stops and entry stops, the market makes some insignificant movement, which has

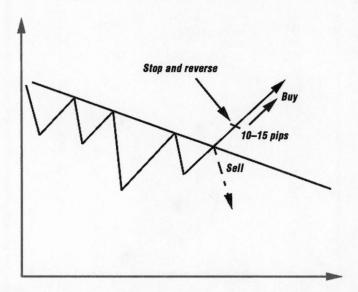

FIGURE 9.4 In case of a break of the trendline, the initial position should be liquidated and reversed.

nothing to do with real follow-through; and then returns without giving the trader an opportunity to realize any profit. Thus the market again crosses a trendline, but from the opposite side. Stops are activated again and the trader loses on two transactions in a row, twice reacting to false signals. Even in this case, traders can still beat the situations using the following technique.

The correctly identified and drawn trendline divides trade space into two parts. Usually, the market doesn't allow such an important line inside the established range. The market shouldn't continue crossing the trendline repeatedly in different directions. Here it will be possible to apply the trading technique based on my method and the principles of money management. Don't allow the market to leave a narrow 20 to 30 pips zone with the trendline going through the middle of it, unless you have a position open in the direction of the current movement of the market. In that case, each time, you should place stops at 15 to 20 pips distance from both sides of a trendline for liquidation of a previous position and open a new position in an opposite direction. See Figure 9.5.

Sooner or later, the market will leave its congestion zone at a distance, sufficient to cover all losses from trade on a choppy market. The only problem might be that something considered sooner for the market, could become too late for a trader. Therefore, you must limit the number

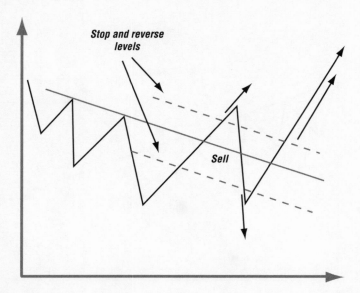

FIGURE 9.5 A false break usually leads to two consecutive trading losses. These could be avoided by applying some intraday trading techniques that allow evaluation of the probability of a false break.

of consecutive losses to three, four, or five and make a decision that depends on the size of the trading contract, size of your account, margin requirements, and strength of your nerves.

There are some other methods of dealing with false breaks, including methods of definition of their probability and also some other approaches using money management. We will talk about these later, in Part V. In any case, you always have to assume that any break of any trendline can be a false one.

I devoted a separate chapter of the course to different strategies in case of a false break of various trendlines, necklines, technical formations, borders, supports, and resistances.

Because in this chapter we talk only about the trendlines angled to the horizon, there is one important detail you have to pay special attention to: The signal to enter the market at the break of the trendline is valid only when the market breaks the ascending supportive trendline or descending resisting trendline. When the market breaks a rising resistance or falling support, you have to react to such a signal with the caution of the great probability that the break will become a false one. See Figure 9.6a and b.

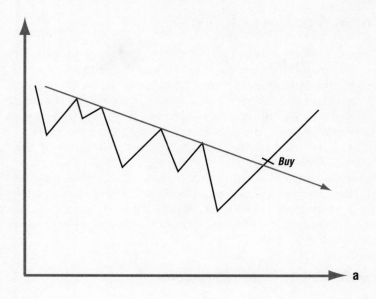

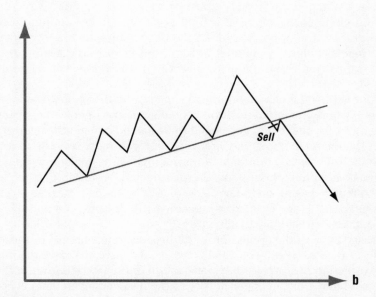

FIGURE 9.6 Figures 9.6 a and b show that if multiple unsuccessful attempts to break a trendline are seen, then a trade plan should be based on entering the market on the break of such a trendline.

TRADING BASED ON CHANNELS

The formation of the channel on the charts of any time frame indicates to me an opportunity to make a profitable trade. The channel is one of my favorite technical formations because I can easily define the degree of risk, which also can be supervised easily during a trade. The channel gives a clear view of the size of the potential profit. When I receive signals from the channel formation, the risk/reward ratio (RRR) exceeds the average RRR that I have when I make transactions on signals received from other sources. See Figure 9.7a and b.

There are three types of channels: ascending, descending, and horizontal. They are often formed on short-term intraday charts and are good just for a short-term trade. Channels are present on daily and weekly charts, too, but as a part of a long-term trend, their borders frequently are a bit dim.

Ascending and Descending Channels

Trading on signals given by channels on the charts does not differ much from trading on the recommendations of technical traders, and it is similar to the principles of trade on ascending and descending trendlines. A trading cycle usually starts from the lower border of the ascending channel, by opening a long position and by opening a short position from the upper border of the descending channel. Stops need to be placed behind a channel border, and in case the stops are activated, a position in an opposite direction (stop and reverse) could be opened.

A target for the channel trading is an area on the opposite side of the channel, where the initial position is liquidated and opens a new position in the opposite direction. Stops need to be placed outside the nearest border of the channel; but if they are activated, you must reverse your position only if there are additional confirmations and signals about possible continuation of the market move in the selected direction. The profit will then be realized again on the opposite side of a channel, then the cycle repeats again up to the moment when stops will be activated and the position will turn in the opposite direction.

Penetration of the upper border of the ascending channel or the lower border of the descending channel is not a valid signal to enter the market in the direction of a break. Only penetration of the lower border of the ascending channel or the upper border of the descending channel is a sufficient signal for opening a position in the opposite direction from a channel. See Figure 9.8a and b.

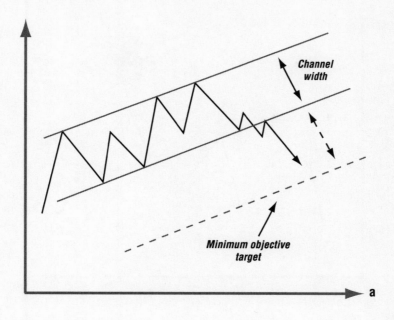

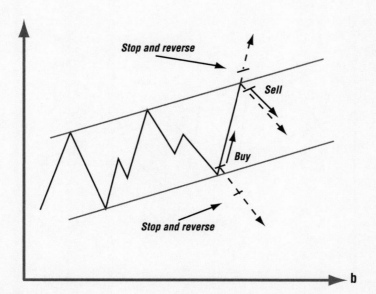

FIGURE 9.7 Channels are some of my favorite patterns. They always are obvious on the charts and provide opportunities to trade in both directions, with measured objective targets and tight stops.

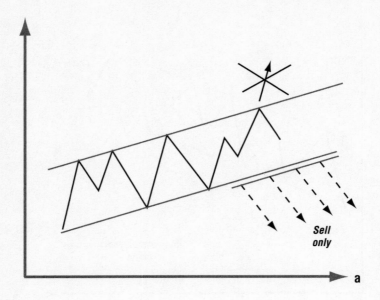

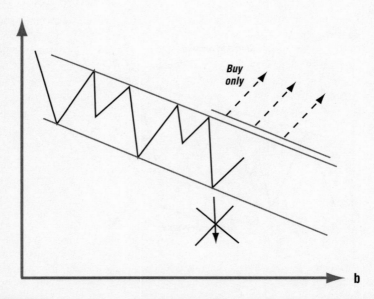

FIGURE 9.8 I never start my trading by entering the market on the break of the upper border of an ascending channel and the lower border of a descending one, if there are no other additional signals received at the moment.

Horizontal Channel

Ideal (or almost ideal) horizontal channels are very rare on long-term charts, but they can be seen on the intraday charts. They are best seen on five-minutes to one-hour charts, or even on a four-hours chart. Because such a channel is formed by two horizontal lines, drawing through at least three points each (according to market laws mentioned earlier), both lines most likely will be broken in the near future.

My experience shows that:

- In the overwhelming majority of cases, the first break of a channel is false.
- After the break, there is a minor move in the same direction, then the market comes back inside the channel.
- After returning into a channel, the market crosses it and penetrates an opposite border.
- After the second break, there is a significant follow-through, which usually exceeds the width of the channel.

Some of my templates are based on signals given by a horizontal channel formation. They will be discussed in Part IV, devoted to intraday trades. The choice of a trade tactic in the formed horizontal channel depends mainly on individual preferences of each trader rather than on the market condition, which basically repeats the same scenario just described, with few variations. Any essential deviations are very rare, but they are possible. When I speak about trader's individual preferences, I have in mind the trader's desire to accept additional risk for an opportunity to gain greater profit. That depends on the degree of his conservatism, time invested in market supervision, individual experience, and speed of reaction to a specific situation.

TRADING BASED ON OTHER TECHNICAL FORMATIONS

I use trade signals given by various technical formations a bit differently from the usual manner accepted in classical technical analysis.

Head and Shoulders (H&S)

H&S is the most recognized reversal technical formation and is very popular among beginners. Many novice traders can see H&S even if there is not even a trace of it on a chart. Seeing H&S where it does not exist occurs not only because of someone's bright imagination but also because of insufficient knowledge of the basics of technical analysis. The alteration of waves in the market occurs constantly, and practically any sequence of contradictory movements can erroneously be interpreted as H&S. This mistake often happens when a trader has an open position and is searching for additional confirmations of his point of view. Wishful thinking can play a malicious joke on a trader, and this actually happens rather frequently.

Therefore, before you apply technical signals related, for example, to H&S, learn to identify the formation first. In all textbooks of technical analysis, there are remarkable pictures showing how this formation should look. Therefore, I recommend that all readers refresh their memories about the shape of H&S, and do not digress from the standard description of the formation. When you have any doubts about unequivocal identification of a formation at the practical trade, it is better not to consider the formation as such. The formation can pretend to be real, if at least nine or ten traders are able to identify it. See Figure 9.9.

However, all obvious formations have one basic and obvious defect that the overwhelming majority of traders can see. Because you cannot expect to take a lot of money from the minority of the market participants (in this case, those who are not capable of identifying the formation for some reason), then complications are most likely to arise. This paradoxical defect requires a solution.

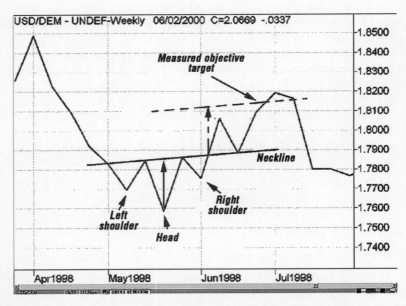

FIGURE 9.9 To illustrate different thoughts and ideas, I'm using the same picture of the inverted H&S formation over and over again, because this one has a perfect textbook-like look that is unusual in the real market. Ten out of ten traders would recognize it.

On the one hand, technical analysis recommends that a trader open a new position in the direction of the market's movement at the break of a neckline. On the other hand, under market laws, the crowd that thinks alike always should lose. The conclusion is: the probability of the correct (i.e., textbook) scenario of the H&S formation should not exceed 50 percent; for this reason, a trader has no statistical advantage, no matter how he acts in a similar situation.

The exit from an inconvenient situation is rather simple. First, because the neckline is a critical line, it is possible to apply a money management system such as the one already described in the example of trendlines, and use stops with reverse to achieve a desirable result. Then, you have to wait until the market leaves a critical zone going in one or the other direction. Secondly (and I frequently apply this method), you can play in advance of the situation and open a new position before such a formation is fully developed. In the case of H&S, I prefer to take a new position at the point I expect to see a potential second shoulder top. The point of a potential second shoulder top is determined by drawing a line parallel to the neckline through the top of the first shoulder, which is already formed.

In the case of inverted H&S, such an entry point will be a possible low of the second shoulder. Stops have to be placed according to intraday supports and resistances, but they can also be placed on some fixed distance from the opening position determined according to scale and size of this particular formation. Such an approach requires some practical experience, but it is easy to learn. All you need to do in such case is pay attention to the situation and keep it under control at all times.

Double Top (Bottom)

In this formation, my recommendations on a trade is the same as in the case of the H&S formation, but only in the part related to entry in the market on the break of a neckline. Don't take a position without completion of the second top (bottom) because it is not always possible to define precisely a point of entry into the market. Sometimes this formation deviates from a horizontal axis of coordinates and inclines on the side. My view is not different from the recommendations of classical technical analysis: protect yourself from a false break by placing relatively tight stops and reversing the position if stops are triggered.

Triangles and Triangle-like Formations

In technical analysis, various triangle-like formations, including wedges, have various names and definitions. According to technical analysis, the market behaves differently after completing the formation of each specific type. Because false signals and fraudulent movements are frequent, it's hard to predict where the market will go after a break of a border of the formation. Anyway, a triangle or any other similar formation almost always allows a trader to make a profitable transaction without dependence on any other reasons and circumstances. When trading triangles, I don't bother to think if this is a continuation or a reversal type formation. My approach to triangles is rather simple.

First, very frequently there is an opportunity of early identification of a triangle after two highs and two lows are formed, through which it is possible to draw lines that supposedly will then become borders of a triangle. Early identification of the triangle allows making 1 to 2 trades inside this formation by opening positions from the bottom/top side in the direction of an opposite side, which will be the target. As the market reaches one side, liquidate the position, take profit, and open a position in the opposite direction, already having the opposite side of the formation as a target. In both cases, stops should be placed outside the formation and on both sides if the triangle is a narrow one. See Figure 9.10.

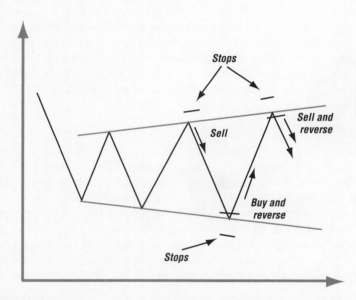

FIGURE 9.10 The broadening triangle is the only formation I really dislike. It looks obvious in the figure, but in reality it is very hard to identify before it is built completely. Most of my own irreversible losses can be attributed to this pattern, which is relatively rare. Only a third approach to one of the borders gives a useful and recognizable signal to enter the market in the direction opposite to the most current trend.

Usually a real break comes after the market has already touched each of the sides three times. (Sometimes it happens even later, on the fourth or fifth touch, but there is no need to wait so long.) After making trades inside a triangle, from one side and to another, simply wait for fourth (or subsequent) touch of one of the sides and open a position in the direction of a movement after the market breaks out from the formation. See Figure 9.11. Here again, you can be trapped by an unpleasant and unexpected false break. In case of a false break, the position should be liquidated when the market returns inside a triangle. The profit should be taken at the level projected from the break point and at the distance equal to the triangle height. See Figure 9.12.

The second interesting factor of dealing with triangle-like formations is that, actually, a false break is in many cases even better for a trader than a real one. It arms him with a high degree of probability to forecast the further course of events, because a false break is nothing else but a perfect confirmation of the market choosing the opposite direction for its next sizeable move. See Figure 9.13.

The false break of a triangle border in the majority of cases is an excellent confirmation of further market intentions. It indicates the future

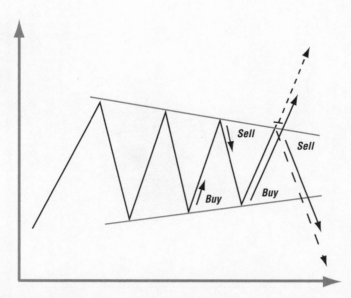

FIGURE 9.11 There shouldn't be a problem trading on a triangle-like formation. Everything is obvious, and a trader can start by entering a position toward one of the borders (heading inside) or on the break of any border (heading outside). Choosing a point to place stops is also an easy task.

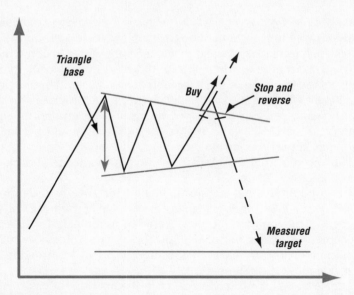

FIGURE 9.12 There is also no problem calculating in advance where to take a profit in the case of trading triangles.

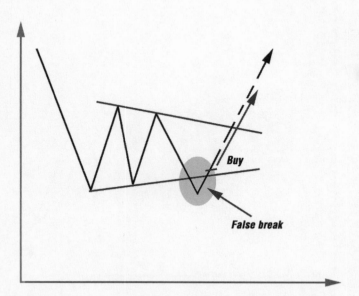

FIGURE 9.13 Trading option in case of a false break of the triangle.

market direction, opposite of the false break. A false break in one direction allows the trader to make the assumption that the market again will cross the triangle and most likely will then reach the objective target, which can be calculated easily.

We will discuss the use of a triangle as a base for construction of trade plans, in Part V.

OTHER FORMATIONS WITH PRECISE BORDERS

Rectangles, flags and some other formations from the theory of technical analysis have the advantage of precisely outlined borders. These borders can and should be used as critical levels, such as supports and resistances. If the width of a particular formation is sufficient, then it is possible to trade inside it, from one border to another. After breaking any one of formation sides, the position should be reversed.

The false break of a formation with a precise border is good, as was mentioned in the case with triangles, and the technique of trading is practically the same.

Rounded Top (Bottom) and V-Formation

In spite of the fact that these two formations look beautiful and obvious in pictures in technical analysis textbooks, I have not found practical application for them in my method. The absence of precise borders in such formations doesn't allow you to plan in advance a trading tactic and then use it. It is almost impossible to receive a true signal about when to enter the market at a certain level and nor do these formations define where to place stops. These formations more often become obvious only when all the events have already taken place and it's already too late to do something about it.

Sometimes more reliable signals to open a position appear, and even acceptable levels for stops form inside such formations. In other cases it is possible to catch these movements, as I did a few times. The trader who reacts to a signal not connected with a basic formation signal, or by accident happens to be in the right place at the right time, feels deeply self-satisfied and wise. I have no objection to feeling satisfaction, but there is no wisdom in such an event.

You never know nor can you predict where the market will go next, and you should never forget this.

CHAPTER 10

Choosing a Currency Pair to Trade

W hen making a choice of a currency pair for a trade, no other reasons except the practical ones should be taken into consideration. It always surprises me when I see that some traders choose a currency pair for making a speculative trade, based on patriotic or geographical reasons. I have noticed that many traders from Australia, for example, basically trade an AUD against USD or NZD. New Zealanders, Canadians, Frenchmen and traders from many other countries frequently prefer to trade their national currencies also. They trade it against the American dollar, or against other national currencies of neighboring countries of the given geographical region. It seems to me, however, that our basic purpose of participation in this business is not to certify our patriotic feelings and pride but to receive the greatest possible profit. From the point of view of a speculative trader, the patriotically geographical approach to a choice of currency pairs for speculative operations on FOREX cannot be considered rational and justified. The choice of a currency pair for the following speculative transaction should be done according to certain parameters, and patriotism and residence are not among them.

The basic criteria for a choice of currency pairs should be their liquidity, activity, and average amplitude of fluctuations (trading range). The higher all these parameters, the more preferable such currency pairs are from a speculative trader's point of view. The list of currency pairs most suitable to such a definition, first of all, includes the following: USD/CHF, USD/JPY, EUR/USD, EUR/JPY, GBP/EUR, GBP/JPY, and CHF/JPY. You may be surprised that I have not included in this group Cable (GBP/USD). The reason is that this currency pair has almost ideal liquidity as well as all other majors, but the average day amplitude of Cable fluctuations is lower than would be desirable. Also, the small cost of a GBP/USD pip is, from my point of view, better for an intermediate term positional trade than for short-term intraday speculations. (I sometimes trade it, but not very often.)

The most important and final criterion when making a choice of a currency for short-term speculative trade should be maximum conformity of a current technical picture, and how it fits to a trading technique and/or to a trading system that you are going to use. Because in this book we talk particularly about my trading technique, just the maximum conformity of the chart to one of the templates used by me becomes a determining factor for a choice of a particular currency for a particular trade. It is especially important if, in the given moment, the market is in immediate proximity to some key technical level.

I accept diversification and, from my point of view, it is possible and necessary to trade various currency pairs. However, my personal practice shows that having simultaneous positions on various currency pairs disseminates a trader's attention. It's rather difficult to follow all the currency pairs at the same time. Therefore, I simultaneously hold open positions on no more than two or (very seldom) three currency pairs. In some cases (for example, trading USD/CHF and EUR/USD), I frequently use substitution. By *substitution* I mean analyzing one of them, but (on the basis of this analysis) trading the other one.

The Swiss franc basically doesn't have its own brightly expressed identity in the marketplace. On a large scale, it is not more than a proxy in relation to Euro. At the same time, it has high activity, large amplitude of fluctuations, and perfect liquidity. These characteristics allow USD/CHF to be one of the most attractive currency pairs for speculative trade.

CHAPTER 11

Money Management Rules and Techniques

Money management is a major component of speculative trade. None of the traders can be successful and none of the trade systems can exist without it. The basic predestination of money management is to preserve and to protect a trading account against possible excessive losses.

Money management's purpose is to control the risk and distribution of investment capital so that one loss or even a series of consecutive losses should not result in the inability to continue a trade, and would not destroy a trading account by bringing it to an unmanageable condition. In a more comprehensive sense, money management also means a technique of preserving current profit in an open position and a technique of fixing current profit.

Plenty of literature is devoted to money management, in which authors with a large amount of practical experience in trading mainly share their thoughts and recommendations about the best approach to manage capital.

Their recommendations in general deserve attention but, unfortunately, numerous publications on this subject agree on only one thing: money management is absolutely necessary for a trader, because it is impossible to expect any success without it. However, when it comes to practical advice and recommendation, we see a large variety of opinions sometimes directly contradicting one another. Therefore, it is difficult to understand these contradictions when reading the works of different authors.

It is almost impossible to choose only one correct approach to correspond to a trader's individual situation, his trade system, the current market condition, and a concrete currency pair. Most important of all, however, is the fact that practically all recommendations about money management basically are directed to a long-term positional trade and not much to what would fit an intraday short-term trade. Therefore, my recommendations will now have a common characteristic: practical suggestions on money management in each of the trading templates intended for an intraday trade.

Because all components of a trade strategy and tactics are connected, some repetition of information will occur.

There are five basic principles of my approach to questions of money management and they are outlined in the sections that follow.

THE MAJORITY OF A TRADER'S MISTAKES CAN BE CORRECTED, AND LOSSES CAN BE COMPENSATED, IF YOU HAVE CORRECTLY CHOSEN MONEY MANAGEMENT TACTICS AND STRATEGY

This principle directly follows from the first two postulates of my method—that the market has only two possible directions of movement and it moves all the time. In reality, if the market moves against an open position, the immediate compensation of losses is possible most of the time if you liquidate an unprofitable position and open a new one in an opposite direction. Doing this at the right place at the right time will provide you some additional comfort and should allow you to cover your losses relatively soon. If you place stops, you will be able to get fast compensation of prime loss, assuming that the loss isn't large enough to keep you from further participation in the market.

This technique works especially well on an intraday trade, according to the third postulate of my method. Because the average daily range on a particular currency pair is usually well-known in advance, it shouldn't be too difficult to calculate whether the market still has potential to cover the initial loss completely or partially. This approach can easily be used in practice. The details of such a technique will be described in Part V of this book.

(During an intermediate or long-term trade, the third postulate plays only an auxiliary role and the reverse technique is a bit different.)

THE TRADER'S PLANS TO RESTRICT THE LOSS FOR A SINGLE TRADE MUST NOT BE CONSTRUCTED ON THE BASIS OF A FIXED PERCENTAGE OR SUM FROM THE TOTAL SIZE OF A TRADING ACCOUNT

Only the market itself can offer a trader the time and place at which an unprofitable position should be liquidated. The trader's only right is to agree or to deny this market's offer. Therefore, stops should be tied to the market's technical levels instead of to a certain amount that the trader considers safe to lose in one trade. The market level at which the position will be liquidated and loss will be accepted should be planned in advance and be a part of the initial trading plan. A trader always has to have a certain limit of loss affordable in any given situation, and the amount must also be calculated in advance. If the nearest technical level suitable for placing stops is outside the limit of acceptable loss, then you should postpone your trade or cancel it altogether. Then, wait until the market comes close enough to such levels or forms a new one, allowing you to place stops on your position within the limits of an acceptable loss.

A TRADER SHOULD ALWAYS HAVE SUFFICIENT CAPITAL RESERVE IN CASE A SINGLE LOSS OR SERIES OF CONSECUTIVE LOSSES TAKES PLACE

You should establish your own restrictions on the margin and volume of the contracts you trade, irrelevant to your dealer's or broker's policy. These restrictions have a direct relation to an overtrade situation. A trade with the margin of 10 to 20 percent seems optimum to me. For example, on each $10,000 to $20,000 of capital in the trading account, you can have just one open contract at a rate of no more than $100,000. The risk of excessive losses within a short period of time will be considerably limited if trading on such conditions. At the same time, sufficient use of capital will still allow you to make a profit, sufficient compared to the total account size. This is so even for an intraday trade.

AVERAGING IS ONE OF THE MOST DANGEROUS TRADING TECHNIQUES FOR USE IN REAL TRADING

Averaging is the most difficult method to control from the money management point of view, and it can be recommended only in isolated cases. I don't recommend it for beginners with small trading capital at all. Averaging is an enemy of money management and the main reason for complete loss of a trading account for the majority of traders who have already vanished from this business.

Averaging is the trading technique of adding a new position to already existing ones that have some floating loss on them. All the positions are on the same currency pair and are open in the same direction. Basically, averaging means that all the positions are open against the prevalent market movement. In many cases, this also means that even having proof of his own mistake, a trader still continues to insist on his wrong opinion. See Figure 11.1.

The main problem of this method is that, in the overwhelming majority of cases, averaging is not part of trader's consciously chosen initial plan, strategy, or tactics. It is rather compulsive steps taken because events on the market have begun to develop a situation not stipulated by a trader. Things just went wrong.

Speculators who find themselves in such a position against their will usually were led to it by one or more of the following reasons:

- greed
- lack of sufficient trading experience
- unwillingness or inability to recognize their own mistakes
- naive belief that the market always comes back
- reliance on their forecast
- belief in their own infallibility
- hope that a bit later, the market will let them liquidate positions at a break even point; and so on

The largest losses among individual traders-investors and among managers of large investment funds are most often connected with an application like averaging. Certainly, the institutional investors have other

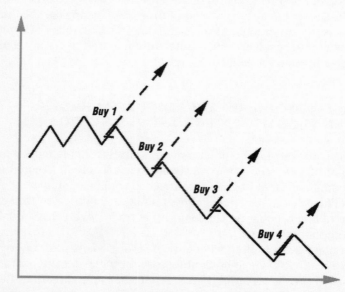

FIGURE 11.1 This simple illustration is just a reminder of how insisting on a wrong opinion can ruin someone's account and future trading career.

reasons for having devastating losses different from those common for individual speculators. These are usually mistakes related to the definition of a force of a long-term trend and, as a consequence, an incorrect money management strategy. There are lots of examples of such losses—Barings Bank, Long Term Capital Management, Tiger Fund, and Quantum Fund, just to name a few victims.

As you can see, even very large capital does not guarantee against losses due to mistakes in money management, especially using such tactics as averaging.

Later, I shall explain the basic principles of positional trade strategy construction using this technique.

RISK/REWARD RATIO (PROFIT/LOSS RATIO) SHOULD NOT NECESSARILY BE CONSIDERED EVERY TIME YOU OPEN A NEW POSITION

It is widely accepted among traders that the ratio between potential profit and probable loss always should be more than 1. This issue may also be related to money management. If you accept this ratio from a mathematical point of view, it gives you an equal number of profitable and unprofitable trades (without mentioning possible additional losses from commissions, slippage, and other operational costs). In other words, it means that each position should satisfy the following condition: Risk/Reward < 1 or Profit/Loss > 1; they are basically the same.

This type of ratio can be compared to a coin toss in which, each time you win, your opponent pays you more than you pay him when you lose. It is clear that even at the ratio of 50/50 (heads and tail), you guarantee yourself profit on the total of all attempts. Referrals to an RRR in all books, brochures, and training recommendation are always nearly identical, namely, the necessity of a positive ratio for the benefit of reward does not cause doubt for anybody. Moreover, for many traders, the number of unprofitable trades is larger than the number of profitable ones. Success in such cases may be achieved only if the average profit for each profitable transaction exceeds the average loss for each unprofitable trade.

To tell you the truth, such mathematical absolute truths give me strong doubts and suspicions about the excessive simplicity of their conclusions. It seems these absolutes don't have any other interpretation, not only because they are based on mathematics, but also because they are easily accepted as true even from the position of common sense. However, the first opinion seems to me to be the wrong one.

When I developed this book, I made a vow to make it as simple and clear as possible to be understood by a person of any level of knowledge

and degree of preparation in an area not connected with trading. Therefore, my basic purpose is to give my students an opportunity to acquire
and to develop practical trading skills, being guided by just ordinary common sense, without stuffing their heads with excessive formulas and theoretical calculations. In this case, I also try to avoid an excessively academic
approach and to simplify my point of view.

It seems to me that the supporters of the obligatory condition,
Risk/Reward < 1, in real trading make some basic mistakes:

First, they consider each trade as an independent event, assuming
that the probability of the profit or loss reception in each concrete case is
50/50. If we agree with this, then the decision to open a position each time
really could be based on simply flipping a coin. Moreover, the 3 step elementary mechanical system should work in this case:

1. Flipping a coin at the beginning of a day (or at any other time), you
   decide to open a position.

2. On a certain fixed distance from the opening price, place a stop that
   has to limit your possible losses.

3. On the opposite side, on a fixed distance, place profitable liquidation
   stops on such a condition that this distance is more than the distance
   from the opening price to a stop loss placement.

A very simple and effective system will guarantee profit if you assume
that the probability of the market movement in one direction or the other
is identical at any given moment. It is clear that, in reality, nobody trades
like this—including the RRR supporters.

Second, you should look at a trade not as a set of unconnected and independent events, but as a process that has its own duration of time and
consists of several consecutive steps of the prepared plan of a trade in accordance with the system of probability estimation. It is clear that, in that
case, the probability of fulfillment of a profitable transaction is greater
each time than the probability of a loss, and constantly changes with the
flow of time. If you insert in the trade one more variable component (for
example, change contract size in the same series of trades inside a trading
plan), the observance of RRR principles becomes senseless.

If we digress from a theoretical discussion and look at real trading, we
shall see that in many cases it's not easy to define the point of liquidation
of a profitable position, that is, to have a target on every single trade. The
absence of a target makes calculation of RRR impossible.

In conclusion, I need to add that neglecting principles of money management will sooner or later cause a catastrophe for a trader.

CHAPTER 12

Market Behavior and Trader Discipline

Psychology of trading and trading discipline are issues of primary importance for a trader. As I mentioned earlier, my desire to reduce psychological stress urged me to create a discrete-systematic trading method.

Because there is plenty written on the subject of crowd psychology, market psychology, and trading psychology, I don't want to repeat those banal and well-known truths of authors who already have written enough on these subjects. I'm essentially against citing any other peoples' opinions, and prefer to think and analyze everything myself. Reading those books, I have noticed that the authors usually have no problem diagnosing traders' common problems, but each writer offers his or her own unique solution. Sometimes, such a solution looks even worse than the problem itself. I have a strong feeling that some advice and recommendations that I have found can cause mental illness in even a previously healthy personality. It's a well-known fact that psychiatrists frequently become similar to their patients after long-term clinical work, and that is why their recommendations look strange from the point of view of an ordinary person.

I assume that all of us are mentally normal adults, and we shouldn't be engaged in personal psychoanalysis discussions. Because of this, I shall limit myself to only a few comments and recommendations about psychological issues. My trading method should offer reliable protection against excessive emotional pressure and stresses, and I hope you soon will be convinced of this.

As I imagine, it would be much more useful and practical for traders to understand from the very beginning the nature of the business that they participate in. After this, traders can develop a correct model of their behavior and their personal attitude to the trading process and to the market in general.

Resolving many problems (both practical and psychological) connected with trading is impossible without precise understanding of the market structure and its propelling forces and character. Problems arise, not by themselves, but as reflections of specific conditions that speculators work in. All these are features of the phenomenon we call the market. The mutual relations of traders and the market are complex, and I think it is wise to try to understand some of these relationships.

I think that, before making a decision to participate in the market, you should correctly imagine what the potential problems are and how to avoid some widespread delusions, which are typical for the majority of beginners. As a treatment should begin with a correct diagnosis, the solution to problems that traders will come across should begin with the formulation and definition of the problems. A trader's psychology and the importance of his emotional self-control were already mentioned in one of the early chapters of this book. Now, we will investigate problems of behavior and mutual relations of the market and traders in more detail.

WHAT IS THE MARKET FROM THE POINT OF VIEW OF A SPECULATIVE TRADER?

I am not going to tell you common truths such as what the market is and how it works. There is plenty of information on the formal side of speculative business that you can get in any book or brochure devoted to FOREX, and also on numerous sites on the Internet. I want to offer you my personal vision of speculative trade problems. It seems to me that my version of an explanation of the market and specific features of a trader's profession (though not indisputable) is worthwhile.

Two independent subjects have and always will be objects of discussions: the model of the market and the predictability of the market.

MODEL OF THE MARKET

A market is a situation in which there is a lack of cooperation of participants that results in constant and unpredictable fluctuations of the exchange rates.

For a long period of time, I was intrigued by the question of how to define the market—what it may be compared with, and how to best describe it. Reflecting on this theme, I suddenly remembered an old event. Many years ago, I witnessed an interesting scientific experiment devoted to questions of family cooperation and the ability of spouses to work together in order to achieve their objectives. One of the tasks was organized as follows:

Couples were divided and sent to two separate rooms so they could not exchange words or communicate with one another in any way. They couldn't see one another, either. In both rooms there was a rheostat, which was attached to a common electrical network. Each of the spouses could control voltage in the network on a scale of the voltmeter installed near each rheostat. Both spouses were operating with only one's own rheostat and change of voltage in an electrical network, without coordination of their actions. The goal was to bring the pointers on the voltmeter scales to a certain fixed position by coordinating both spouses' efforts.

As far as I remember, only one couple out of 20 succeeded. The husband shot the pointer of the voltmeter to an extreme position, thus giving his wife an opportunity to quietly make the necessary adjustment and to bring the pointer of her device into the required position. All the other couples didn't make it, because (despite a common goal) they couldn't coordinate their actions enough in order to complete the task. Every time, the pointer of the device passed through the required position and couldn't be fixed, because each of the participants of the experiment acted according to his or her own ideas and did not consider the actions of their partners.

PREDICTABILITY OF THE MARKET

The question of predictability of the market always was and always will be one of the primary discussions among speculative traders. Traders will argue if and how it is possible to forecast the market. As the absolute majority of traders are engaged in forecasting, it is not difficult to come to the conclusion that the common opinion of the majority is that the market can be predicted. There are many market analysts offering their services and selling their own analyses and forecasts to traders. This fact speaks in favor of forecasting, too. At the same time, I constantly hear many of my fellow traders complaining that market behavior frequently contradicts fundamental economical or political realities.

The result of correct guessing of market reaction to economical or political changes is no better, and may be even worse, than flipping a coin in order to make a decision. Similarly many traders try to predict the future behavior of a market only on the basis of technical analysis and with approximately the same result. At the same time, it would be wrong to insist that the market should ignore events and factors of fundamental character when they definitely are its main driving force. It seems to me that the basic reason for disharmony between an event and consequences of this event is that the fundamental factors influence the market not directly, but rather they are refracted through the market participants' perception.

Let's make a short list of three possible reasons for a so-called wrong market behavior:

1. Different traders interpret the same fundamental factors differently.

2. The intents of various market participants are different, as well as reasons and purposes of conducting a transaction. Reasons may include hedging, purchase of currency with the purposes of financing the international commercial project, or a bargain for a speculative profit.

3. As the market is simultaneously influenced by the various fundamentals and contradictory forces, the final reaction can vary, causing fluctuations of the market, and not comply with the expected reaction to some fundamental event or process.

I have my own explanation about the unpredictability of the market, and its discrepancy to the fundamentals.

Despite the opinions spread among traders, the main market participants—banks and other financial institutions involved in speculative operations on FOREX—aren't extraordinary at all. The large participants are not many-headed dragons, offending the weak and taking away money from small speculators, as they are frequently represented to a beginner. Besides the fact that they move huge capital in the marketplace and their transactions cause movement of the market (and hence, significant change of the exchange rates), those people are pretty ordinary individuals. Hence this capital is moved by ordinary people with common weaknesses. They have no special ability to see the future, and they make serious and sometimes even fatal mistakes as well. Bankruptcy of such whales of the financial world as Barrings Bank, Long Term Capital Management Fund and Tiger Fund, which have taken place in the past, are examples of traders' mistakes resulting in fatal consequences and ruining formerly mighty financial structures.

It is quite possible that some movements of the market are provoked by such erroneous transactions. A few years ago, I found interesting statistics, according to which the average career of an institutional trader lasts only about four to five years. After that, people either leave for higher positions not related to trading, or completely change their career. For such a short period of time, it is impossible to become a true professional, so I have come to the conclusion that many dilettantes play on the market, causing all its difficult-to-explain fluctuations with many different consequences.

HOW TO TREAT THE MARKET

To develop the correct attitude to a market will require some time and efforts spent on psychological training. You have to accept the fact that the life experience you had when you decided to become a trader is absolutely useless and even harmful to your new profession. This should become the first and most important step in your psychological preparation. If you belong to the majority of mankind (i.e., have normal mentality and standard reaction to irritants), then in market conditions your experiences and ability to think with common sense will not help you. Your standard way thinking will automatically put you with a majority that thinks exactly the way you do. Unfortunately, because of the way the market is arranged, each time you join the crowd, you will definitely lose.

There is a simple and logical explanation that is clear at the common-sense level, but not everything associated with common sense is as simple as it seems. It is assumed that everyone has common sense, including you and me. However, what we call common sense often happens to be an illusion, a simplification, or a political correctness that has no direct connection to common sense. These illusions and politically correct assumptions help us to live in a society and make us similar to others, but for trading in the market, they will work against us in the long run.

The majority of traders in the market are always wrong, and the most common and widespread opinions about the future market are (in the prevailing majority of cases) incorrect. Conclusions and choices made by a crowd are always wrong and lead to money losses in speculative trading operations. To avoid possible disappointments, it will be useful for beginners to remember the following three basic postulates:

1. Try to have no opinion concerning the future market's behavior. Trade only according to your trade system and only on signals that the market itself gives you.

2. Try to avoid wishful thinking. If you have an open position, first of all pay attention to the trading signals that contradict your point of view, instead of those that confirm it.

3. Listen attentively to other traders' opinions. Share your ideas with colleagues on Internet forums and in personal dialogues. If half of your colleagues-traders approve your idea, double your vigilance. Check up and analyze the situation once again, looking for a possible mistake. If you have found that the absolute majority of traders share your point of view, immediately abandon your initial plan of trading and make a new one. In the new plan, you should assume that the market most likely would choose an opposite direction. The absolute

disagreement of the majority with your opinions on current events in the market is additional and valuable confirmation of the correctness of your position. Such confirmation should give you an additional reliance on the correctness of your decision.

The basic conclusion a trader should make is that, because the market is not predictable, it doesn't pay to be engaged in predicting and forecasting its behavior. The absence of forecast and, accordingly, opinion will have a positive effect on a trader's mindset. Such an approach relieves the trader of the need to admit mistakes and to experience stress and disappointment resulting in it.

Besides this basic conclusion, I offer you some recommendations on how a trader should think so that problems of human psychology have no negative effect on the trader's work.

Concerning the Market

- None of the experience, mindset, ability, and success of a trader in other kinds of activity is a guarantee of success in the trading profession.
- Common sense does not work in speculative trading in the market.
- Almost everything that you assume about the market does not correspond with reality.
- Everything a majority of market participants consider obvious is actually never that obvious.
- The "more obvious" to a trader current market situation is, the more surprising its further development will be.
- The market always goes against the opinion of a majority.
- If in the past you didn't have the ability to foretell the future, don't have the illusion that you can ever precisely forecast future market behavior.
- Events on the market always develop under the most improbable script, and they never comply with your expectations or with the point of view and forecasts of other participants.
- The market eventually arrives at even the most easily predicted price levels, in the most confusing way.
- Try to predict the future behavior of the market; it is nothing but good gymnastics for your brains. Never trade on your forecasts. You need other tools for this purpose.
- Any market's behavior has a suitable explanation. The reasons for this behavior always become known too late.
- Accept the market as a natural phenomenon that you are not capable of understanding, explaining, or predicting.

Concerning Profit

- The market is not a charitable organization and is not capable of ensuring profit to either a majority or all of its participants.
- Profit received by a trader does not materialize from nowhere, and it is formed at the expense of someone else's losses.
- The market exists only because the redistribution of money always occurs at the expense of the majority of the participants for the benefit of the minority.
- Any position you open can become unprofitable.
- When trading on the market, you should never be 100 percent sure about anything.

THE RECOMMENDATION TO A BEGINNING INDEPENDENT TRADER

You should realize precisely and completely that your trading account is only a tool for making money, but it is not money itself. From the moment your money was placed on the working account as an investment, it lost its usual functions inherent in money as a universal means of payment. This money cannot symbolize your ability to exchange it for a new automobile or to spend it for realization of other boons and pleasures. From this moment, your investment becomes for you only a tool of making money (this time real money, with all the attributes connected to it).

I hope that if you can produce for yourself a similar attitude to the market, work itself will turn into an ordinary and quite routine business for you, without excessive stress.

DISCIPLINE OF TRADING

Always apply discipline to your trading. Without discipline, trading is impossible, and the knowledge you acquire from studying this course is absolutely useless. If you do not find enough strength and discipline and do not consider following all the rigid rules, you would do yourself a favor by leaving this business. Even if you decide to leave the business, I consider this book worthwhile, because such a decision will save you a lot of time and money.

PART IV

Short-Term and Intraday Trading Strategies Using the Igrok Method

Intraday trading—when a position is open and liquidated within one trading day (24 hours)—must be considered as one of the most complicated types of trade and, nevertheless, most widespread among independent individual traders. Its popularity among traders can be explained by some subjective reasons. It might be connected to the small size of investment capital and a trader's desire to receive the greatest possible advantages from margin trading with a large leverage. (As I have already mentioned, the appelation "day trade" is considered an artificial one, because the FOREX market works round the clock, five days a week, and a trader does not have and cannot have obligations to liquidate his positions the same day, even if they have been open without special necessity. Therefore, when I talk about short-term trading, I mean positions held for a period from a few minutes to a few days.)

Short-term trading is considered to be extremely difficult, because its results are greatly influenced by market noises of significant amplitude— sometimes as big as the average amplitude of daily fluctuations. Practically all short-term trading is conducted on market noises, and the trader's problem consists mainly of catching small and medium-sized fluctuations, basically from several pips and up to a couple of hundred pips.

111

The advantages of an intraday trade are obvious. First of all, it is the opportunity to work with small investment capital by taking numerous positions during the day and placing very tight stops. As for profitability, it can also be more profitable than long-term trading but probably not all the time. That closes a very short list of advantages of intraday trading.

All intraday trading's other distinctive features can be defined as passive, because they basically have a negative character. Intraday trading on FOREX differs by high risk, high labor input, long working days, work under constant stress, and chronic weariness. The specific conditions of intraday trading require a speculator's fast reaction, absolute discipline, calmness, and endless patience. However, the real key to success is an effective and reliable trading technique specially created for this type of trading, which would allows a trader to make optimal decisions under the constraints of limited time and market space.

CHAPTER 13

Principles of the Intraday Trading Plan

A ny trade should begin with scheduling, and can't be done without it. The planning of each transaction is very important. Planning helps reduce or even completely eliminates the influence of negative stress factors. It must be done in advance, to prevent the necessity of making important decisions in limited time constraints, when the probability of making mistakes grows exponentially. Planning is absolutely necessary for intraday trading; without it, it would be impossible to have any chance for eventual success.

In addition to the choice of a currency pair, preliminary planning of each intraday trade includes four basic elements. Decisions about them should be made in advance. A trader has to decide the following four things:

1. Where to enter the market with a long or short position;
2. Where to cut loss (where to place a stop-loss order);
3. Where to take profit.
4. Whether a new position will be open in an opposite direction (reverse), in case the stops are triggered.

Having the answers to all four questions prior to the beginning of a trade will make an ideal plan. However, ideal planning in the real market isn't always possible. Frequently, a preliminary plan requires some adjustment because of constantly changing market conditions. It's almost impossible to foresee all the possible situations in advance, and the importance of each separate element of the trade planning is unequal.

Therefore, I follow two main rules:

1. I do not begin a trade if I haven't decided at least the two first elements, and I do not begin to trade if one or both of them are missing from my trading plan.
2. The correction of a preliminary plan can occur only inside a basic, accepted-in-advance trading strategy. For example, some minor details can vary in the plan, but if the plan is already in the process of realization, I can't change it.

The sequence of building a trading plan using the four elements stated above should be done according to the priority which we discuss next. (Elements 3 and 4 of a preliminary plan could be considered less important details of a trading plan.)

RULES AND TECHNIQUES OF STOPS PLACING

The stop levels should be determined in accordance with one of the principles of the method, which states that the market has only two possible directions in which to go. Therefore, stops should be placed only where the probability of continuation of a movement in the direction against your position grows sharply. The stops for liquidation of long positions should be placed at the point where the market gives a signal on opening of a short position. The same is true for the opposite scenario. For this reason, in many cases and according to my strategy, I liquidate a losing position and simultaneously open a new one in the opposite direction.

If for any reason you can't determine a level of placing stops in advance, it is not worth opening a position at all. Such a situation has happened frequently in my practice. The problem basically arises when I search for an opportunity to open a position in the direction opposite to the current market movement. In order to solve this problem, I apply some money management principles and have one more rule to follow: If I cannot find an acceptable level for placing stops in a sufficient proximity from the current market price, I refrain from making a transaction until the market builds to one that will include all the necessary elements. (Because we are talking here about intraday trading, sufficient proximity can be considered any distance anywhere from 20 pips and up to an average daily range of the particular currency pair you are dealing with at the present moment.)

An obligatory condition should be the binding stops to a technically significant level, that is, to support, resistance, or a trendline. Stops should be placed only where the probability of continuation of a movement in the direction against your position grows sharply.

As far as I know, lots of traders usually place stops considering money management reasons only. In such cases, the stops are placed on some fixed distance from a position open price, and typically not further than 30 to 50 pips. Sometimes, traders have some fixed amount in mind that they allow themselves to lose in one trade. Technical levels such as trend lines, supports, or resistances (frequently being close at a short distance behind the stops) are not taken into consideration. Such a practice results in stops that are triggered at the most improper moment. Too frequently, a prospective and potentially profitable position is liquidated and a loss is taken.

To avoid such situations, here is another rule I always follow: Place no stops based on reasons of money management only. The binding of a stop should always be done to a specific technical level. If the nearest suitable technical level lies on a distance more than a trader can afford to lose in one transaction, he should refrain from making a trade until the market comes close enough to such an appropriate level.

In some cases, it might be necessary to open a position against the current market movement because of the opportunity to catch the moment of a market turn. For this purpose, a position needs to be opened near the assumed top or bottom—a task that is very difficult to make with precise accuracy. Then, the technique I call "postponed stops" can be applied. Postponed stops become attached, not to a specific price level, but to some specific time. More often, the postponed stops attach to the end of a trading day, session, or moment when the market finally builds a new, clearly expressed technical level. This is especially true if this new level can become a new top or bottom on which I will be able to put my new stop. Even in these cases, however, I have to be ensured against possible excessive losses and place a safety stop outside a possible range. This range is the level, which the market probably won't achieve at the present time. Usually, I place these stops within the limits of 100 to 150 pips from the price at which my position was opened. A safety stop should also be bound to a certain technical level. I cancel a safety stop when a postponed stop becomes invalid and a suitable technical level at which to place stops is found.

A stop shouldn't be cancelled under any circumstances or a trade be conducted without using stops. A stop can be moved (if necessary) in one direction only—closer to an open position price. In order to preserve a current floating profit, a trailing stop can also be used. When moving stops, you should always place a new one first and then cancel the old one.

CHAPTER 14

Entering the Market

A new position opening technique is the second most important element of preliminary trade planning. The rules of an opening of a new position and entering the market are numerous and require very precise adherence. Because we are discussing intraday trading, the choice of an entry point represents an especially important and difficult task because of the limited time—one day—and limited space—the average daily range of any given exchange rate. First, we should always remember and consider the fact that, during an intraday trade, all trading activity reflects only a market noise. In other words, the result of any single trade is greatly influenced by the casual movements of the market and its chaotic fluctuations of significant amplitude, viewed against an average daily range. Therefore, the tactics that can and should be applied to intraday trading can be characterized as the hit-and-run technique.

HOW TO CHOOSE AN ENTRY POINT

The choice of an entry point should be based on technical signals that are submitted by the market when it comes close to a critical level defined by a trader in advance. According to this rule, a new position opening point should be at the closest possible distance from the technical level that you should define as critical at the present moment.

A certain line drawn on the chart (whether a support or resistance, trendline, or border of some formation) should be considered as the critical level. In some cases, a narrow price range can also be defined as a critical

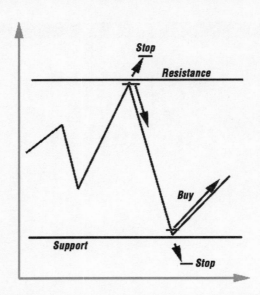

FIGURE 14.1 Commonly known recommendations: Buy ahead of a support and sell ahead of a resistance.

zone; above it, the market submits a buy signal and below it a sell signal. A long position should be opened ahead of a support, and a short position should be opened ahead of a resistance. See Figure 14.1. When done so, the stops should be placed on the opposite side of the line, dividing the market space into two different parts. (Below the line, a short position is preferable; and above the line, go long.)

A new position open price should be at the closest possible distance from the technical level you consider as critical at the present moment.

ENTRY TIMING RULES

There are three rules I follow about when to enter the market:

1. There should be some period of time between the moment of making a decision about opening a new position, and actual transaction execution. This period of time gives a trader an opportunity to reconsider his decision and to abort it if necessary. It also prevents him from making improperly justified and impulsive decisions.

Such an approach guarantees you against making impulsive and insufficient decisions. It will save you a lot of worry and money. The duration of this period can fluctuate from several minutes to several hours. As was already indicated earlier, no transaction can be executed before the levels and conditions of protective stops for a new position are determined. The duration of this period will also give you an opportunity to again reconsider your trading plan and, if necessary, to introduce additional corrective amendments into it. In some cases, such a period of expectation can result in radical changes to the initial plan, and even in its complete rejection.

Often, the same price level gives an opportunity for opening positions in opposite directions within the same trading day. Such conditions often come after the market completely fulfills one trading signal and creates an opportunity for entering the market in the opposite direction. See Figure 14.2.

2. Generally speaking, any position (if open in the direction of the current market's movement) will give a trader an appreciable statistical advantage in the prevalence of profitable trades over unprofitable ones. This advantage amplifies if such a position opens at the moment of highest market activity and greatest speed of the move.

Such a trading tactic is the most conservative and safest one. Even if it seems that such an approach lowers the average size of the potential

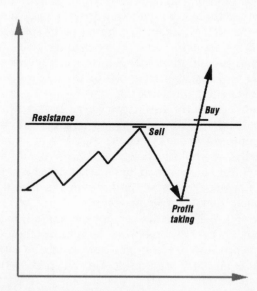

FIGURE 14.2 The market provides an opportunity to make a profitable short trade before going long on the break of the resistance.

profit, it gives a statistical advantage—the prevalence of profitable trades over unprofitable ones. This tactic can also be considered the least stressful because, in most cases, some profit will be generated almost immediately after opening a position.

I open the overwhelming majority (75 to 80 percent) of new positions in the direction of the current movement of the market. The statistics of profitable and unprofitable trades show that the majority of profitable trades are accomplished by opening a position in the direction of the current market movement. I am absolutely sure that if you follow the rule of opening new positions only in the market but not against it, the statistical prevalence of profitable trades over unprofitable ones could be overwhelming.

Planning most trades in advance provides some additional comfort to a trader. In this case, positions can automatically be taken in accordance with the preliminary designed plan at the desired price levels. There will be no need to monitor the market constantly, and, most of the time, I use a limit or an entry stop order for opening the initial position. I do this even if I'm not going anywhere and am only watching the market. There are several advantages to such a trading technique:

- First of all, I'm saving my time, and if the position according to my plan is taken using a limit order, then I can place a protective stop simultaneously. After that (if no reverse was planned), I have nothing to worry about and there is no need to watch the price action at all.
- In case the position is taken through an entry stop order, then all I need to do is set an alarm. When the computer gives me a signal that the order is executed, then I place protective stops and once again have nothing to worry about and can spend my time doing something else besides watching the market.
- Automatic position entry also saves worry. It gives me a feeling that I'm in control of the situation at any moment. I feel myself in charge of the trading process, because I chose the price at which to enter and exit the market, as well as price at which to give up if things turned bad for me. If, for some reason, the market didn't reach my projected price level, I consider it as the market's own problem, and there was no good trading signal or price to enter it.
- Automatic order execution also allows me to enter and exit the market at the exact price I planned from the very beginning, and not to reconsider my previous trading plan too often. In case the position opens through an entry stop order, I'm not missing the move if the market is moving too fast.
- Such a technique also supports my money management requirements and allows me to calculate my potential losses in advance.

I open up to 85 to 90 percent of my positions using this technique, and the overwhelming majority of them are in the direction of the current movement of the market.

3. If, in accordance to a trading plan, the position should be opened in the direction opposite to the most current movement of the market, it would be better to do it during the least market activity and its slowest movement.

Many traders have failed and were compelled to leave business forever because their basic tactics for a trade were mostly based on attempts to catch the moments of the market reverse. It is incredibly difficult to catch the exact moment of change in the trend or the market direction, especially when trading short-term contracts. In longer-term trading, this issue looks a bit easier and can be successfully performed in some cases. Using the common sense trading technique often allows me to catch the price close to extreme with a relatively high degree of success, but it also works well in case my interest at the moment is not higher profit but rather the safest way to make some profit.

Because the trend has high momentum and inertia, the reverse process usually takes a significant period of time. Therefore, it is possible to open positions in the direction opposite to the direction of a previous or current market's movement only when the market calms down a bit and shows signs of inability of further movement in the initial direction. The speed of its movement should be considerably reduced, and the market should be moving sideways before it gives a chance to open a new position. If the market stops moving during some period of time and does not form new local extremes, you can think of opening a new position in the opposite direction. The details will be described in the templates of this book.

4. The most effective trading tactic can be considered the one that assumes a new position opening only in the most probable direction of movement of a day. A good trading plan should never be based on possible retracement of the main move. It's also dangerous to open a new position against the main direction of a day movement, if the market has already determined this direction. The less time remaining until the end of a trading day (24 hours), the less is the probability that the market will suddenly change the direction of the main intraday movement to the opposite.

This recommendation also follows directly from the philosophical concept of the method. First of all, the market is not a sewing machine in which the needle runs up and down with identical amplitude and speed.

Usually, if the market is active enough, it has a highly visible intraday basic direction.

Statistically, before a reversal, there should be a certain period of market hesitation that a trader can use either for liquidation of the profitable position or for planning to open a new position in the opposite direction. However, all this can be correct and will work only when the market has not yet chosen the direction of the main intraday trend, and has not finished formation of a daily trading range. The market also requires some time to reverse and to begin its movement toward the opposite side of the previously established range—especially if there is not much time left before the end of the day and the average amplitude hasn't been seen yet. Therefore, at the opening of new intraday short-term positions, I consider the following rules 5 and 6 useful:

5. Do not open new positions on the European currencies against USD at the beginning of a trading day or during the Asian trading session.

This rule is also connected to the fact that, more often than not, the increase in activity of European exchange rates begins only after the opening of the European trading session. During the Asian session, the rates of European currencies against USD and other non-Asian currencies trade passively, most of the time in a narrow range that demonstrates classical behavior of the market in a narrow side trend. There are rare exceptions to this rule, such as when I consider making a safe short (20 to 40 pips) trade with tight stops and to liquidate the position prior to the beginning of the European session. This situation does not happen very often, and I try to not make many of these trades. From the time when I was an absolutely green novice and traded without stops, I remembered well that the longest lasting positions were targeted for a fast profit. Therefore, I don't recommend such trades to my students (especially beginners), and I don't plan to describe this technology in this book.

The other kind of exception occurs in cases when, during the Asian session, the rate of the European currency reaches some critical level, the definition of which is possible by analyzing the longer-term charts like daily, weekly or monthly. In these cases, it is necessary to react to the signal received, even if such situations happen very rarely.

6. I do not open new positions against the major market move of the day after the beginning of the New York trading session, and especially after ending of the European session.

It is not so difficult to determine where the main movement of a day has been directed. In most cases, it could be clearly seen on the charts by the closing time of the European session. It is characterized by a highly visible intraday trend and also by expansion of the intraday range, which has occurred during the entire previous period of time from the beginning of a current trading day.

The only case in which you can accept some risk and open a new position against the main movement of a day during the New York session is as follows:

- The market has reached one of the main technical levels such as a major support or a major resistance. This level should have more than local intraday significance, but it has to be easily determined on daily charts as a minimum.
- The daily range has already exceeded its average typical range for the particular currency by the time the major technical level was achieved.
- The main move of the day was formed as a result of an impulsive market reaction to someone's comment or market news.

When these conditions are met, there is a possibility for a countertrade with stops placed outside the most current extreme, major support, or resistance zone. However, the probability of making a profitable trade in such a situation does not usually exceed 50 percent.

CHAPTER 15

Exiting the Market

POSITION LIQUIDATION AND PROFIT TAKING

In my trading method, I use several different ways to take profit and to liquidate profitable positions. The choice of one or the other in a real market situation depends on the current technical picture, presence or lack of trading signals, timing, market speed, amplitude and sequence of the previous fluctuations, short- and medium-term trend direction, and such. It's absolutely impossible to describe each and every combination of different factors. Here, I will give you just a few general tips on how and when a profitable position can be squared and profit pocketed.

PROFIT-TAKING AT THE MOMENT YOU RECEIVE A SIGNAL TO OPEN A POSITION IN THE OPPOSITE DIRECTION

At first glance, such a way of trading may seem in general like the ideal one. This way seems like it would allow a trader to stay in the market forever by switching his positions from long to short ones, taking profits and losses, and every time reversing in the opposite direction. However, for a million obvious reasons, such a scenario is almost absolutely impossible, especially if trading on an intraday basis. Even if you exclude such factors as physical impossibility to control the market for the whole day, five days a week, and that more trades usually result in fewer profits, it still

125

wouldn't be reasonable to try to catch every intraday fluctuation. For intraday trading, for example, when a trader has to deal within a limited time frame and market space, a hit-and-run tactic might be considered as the most sufficient and effective. This tactic does not give traders an opportunity to switch from one position to the opposite one, without risking their floating profit every time they wait for a signal to take profit and open a position in the opposite direction.

The average daily range, even on the most volatile and active currencies, doesn't usually exceed 180 to 200 pips. Also, a lifetime of an intraday position rarely lasts more than several hours—and sometimes, even minutes. It is also obvious that in order to complete such a daily range and stay within it for a 24-hour period, the market has to fluctuate inside this range, going up and down through the same levels several times in one day. Thus, we can come to a conclusion that because the market most likely gives the opportunity to enter opposite positions at the same price level but at different moments of the day, a profit-taking tactic based on trading signals cannot be considered as too effective. Of course, there are some exceptions to the rule. I think that the tactics described earlier can be used in such cases as when, during the day, the market approaches major and long-term trendlines, supports, and resistances, and different formations' borders—all of which can be identified on longer-term charts starting with daily. In these cases, traders also have an opportunity not just to liquidate their profitable position, but also to open a new one at the same price but in the opposite direction.

PROFIT-TAKING IF THE MARKET SPEEDS AND ACTIVITY DECREASES

This criterion can also be used as a signal to pocket your profits. Unfortunately, in practice it's not always possible to know exactly if the market activity decrease means that it is getting ready to turn in the opposite direction, or if the initial move will continue after some market hesitation and trading sideways. However, there are some signs that may help you to determine further market intentions. First of all, usually the turn doesn't happen at once. It usually takes some time to change the direction of the move to the opposite. Also, the market usually forms a sharp top or bottom (V-formation) when reaching a real extreme, even if this extreme is a local one and can be seen on an intraday basis. So if the market has formed a sharp top or a bottom and then is trading sideways after some correction, it might be a sign to think about pocketing your profits. If there is a flat surface formed on a very top or a very bottom of the range, then the market will most likely continue its move or at least make some extension in the same direction. See Figure 15.1.

To determine, for an intraday trade, whether the stop of the move is final or not, we should take a look at short-term charts—starting from 5 minutes and up to 15 minutes bar charts. If your position is having a floating profit at the moment and the last extreme has a flat end (top or bottom), then it would be better to wait a bit longer before taking a profit. If the market stops for long and doesn't make a new high (or low) within the period of time equal to that which it took to commit the move, then the position had better be liquidated and profit fixed. This criterion is very simple to apply to real trading. All you need is to count a number of bars on 5-minute intraday charts. If the number of bars after the market formed its last extreme equals or exceeds the number of bars that formed the last wave, then it's time to get out. See Figure 15.2.

FIGURE 15.1 Flat surfaces at the top are illustrated.

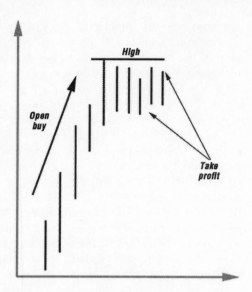

FIGURE 15.2   The number of bars at high are 6. Number of bars after the market formed its last extreme is 4. Time to get out and take profit.

PROFIT-TAKING BASED ON TIMING

This is one of the most simple and reasonable ways to pocket a profit because the market has its own specific cycles of activity. These cycles are changing from time to time, but it's easy to identify a particular one after some watching. Some of those cycles can sometimes be identified on the basis that the market makes extremes at certain periods of time of the day. If such a pattern is seen and proven, then it gives a trader, not just an opportunity to liquidate his position at nearly the best price, but also to take another position in the opposite direction.

The other choice related to timing would be pocketing profit at a certain moment—for example, 30 to 40 minutes before the end of the European session. The profit taking may start when the correction against the main move of the day will begin, or at the very end of a trading day before the closing of the New York session.

PROFIT-TAKING BASED ON AMPLITUDE OF A DAY RANGE

This one should also work pretty well and (at least statistically) makes a lot of sense. By calculating the average day range for the last couple of months (for example), we can easily make a projection for any current day in terms of its possible range. So, the position might be liquidated and profit taken if the market has already reached its average day limits and fully completed its daily task. Such an approach is usually good when a position was taken after the market has already formed some intraday range and the timing (in regards to cyclical changes) is also taken into consideration.

So we have a variety of different approaches to profitable position liquidation, but it is also important to remember that the time frame for each trade should be planned (even roughly) in advance. It would be better to follow the initial plan from the very beginning to the very end, unless some dramatic market changes call for its review and reconsideration.

EXITING A POSITION WITH A SIMULTANEOUS REVERSE

Position liquidation with simultaneous opening of a new one in the opposite direction is a method that I apply frequently. In most cases, I apply it at the moment of liquidation of an unprofitable position, but there are cases in which the reverse occurs at liquidation of a position with profit. Between these two cases, there is a basic difference, and it makes sense to consider each of them separately.

Simultaneously Reverse and Liquidate an Unprofitable Position

Simultaneously opening a new position in the opposite direction and liquidating a previous one is a quite normal and natural action for me. Why not? Things went wrong—not as I was hoping in the beginning while making my trading plan. The market has to go somewhere and there are just two possible directions for that. So I don't hesitate. I had better take a position where the market goes, instead of sitting and doing nothing after the stops were triggered. Because I try not to have an opinion about future market behavior and its direction, I do not feel any stress in relation to liquidation of one position and opening the opposite one. Really, why should I worry if there is a confirmation that the market is choosing the opposite direction and it is possible to earn money trading either way? By receiving confirmation that the market is not going to follow in a direction originally selected in accordance with my initial plan, it would be quite logical to try to achieve success by reversing a position. In such cases, the new position usually opens automatically at the moment the stops trigger. My only concern is that such an action always has to be part of the initial trading plan. Like the rules of stops placing that we discussed, opening a new position at reverse also has to be carried out using similar tactics. However, in order to make a decision to reverse a position, there should be some certain terms and preconditions met to avoid possible problems and complications. There are also some times when the reverse is not recommended because it can be too risky.

The presence of the following factors will favor position reverse, if they occur at the moment of reverse:

- The market breaks a major technical level, which can be determined at the analysis of intermediate- and long-term charts.
- There is an opportunity to place tight stops, and the risk taken doesn't exceed a safe level in case of possible loss.
- The market is active and its speed is high.
- The intraday range is broadening.
- There is an expressed intermediate-term trend in the direction of the newly open position.

The reverse of a position can appear inexpedient and risky if:

- Activity of the market and its speed are rather low.
- The reversed position will be open against the main direction of the day.
- The new position will be directed against the intermediate trend.
- There are less than two hours before the end of a trading day.
- The market has already formed or exceeded its average daily amplitude.
- The point of reverse is not tied to any significant technical level.
- The nearest technical level suitable for placing stops is too far from it and is outside an acceptable range.

These common reasons are not rigid rules, and the decision should be made with regard to the particular situation. Some preliminary analysis and consideration of several possible variations should also be done. In any case, the decision to reverse a position should be made in advance and be part of the whole trading plan from the time the initial position was opened. The reverse is best when you place the stop that will be activated at the same price at which the initial position was liquidated.

Contract Size Increase (Doubling) for a Reversed Position

I apply this method rarely, though it is known that many traders use it widely. It seems to me that, in many cases, there is no practical expediency in such an action. Rather, the incentive is elementary greed, the desire to recoup and to cover losses as soon as possible. More so, increasing contract size is related to psychology rather than to a trader's everyday routine (only in a case when such a practice is not part of a mechanical trading system used by a trader). I think that mistakes or lack of professionalism should not be corrected at the expense of such purely mechanical actions as a contract size increase at the moment of position reversal, because the risk also increases accordingly.

When several consecutive losses during the same trading session occur (for example, a choppy market situation took place), increasing contract size can result in severe damage to the trading account. Therefore, I apply a double contract size at a position reverse only when there is an opportunity to place a very tight stop. More often, I liquidate the surplus in the contract size as soon as the profit covers the initial loss. Besides, I prefer to double a contract size after two consecutive losses only. If a third one happens this time, I stop trading until the next day, when new trading opportunities and signals will be generated.

Reverse at the Moment of Liquidation of the Previous Profitable Position

I use this scheme rarely, but more often than I apply the technique of doubling the contract size. I use it seldom, not because I do not like such an approach, but because such a method requires great accuracy, attention, and certain conditions that need to develop in the market. Unfortunately, in practice, the conditions for this kind of trade are rare, especially for intraday trading.

The reverse with simultaneous liquidation of a profitable position is possible under two circumstances:

1. The market reaches a strong technical level that it is unlikely to pass.
2. The market gives a signal for opening a position in the opposite direction.

In both cases, a trade execution can be made directly by a trader through a market order, whether he looks after the market at this moment or it is done automatically. The automatic order occurs when an old position is liquidated through a limit order at the level calculated in advance, that is, directly ahead of strong technical support or resistance. A new position then opens simultaneously by the same order. Externally, it looks like an ordinary limit order but twice the size of the initial contract. In both variations, stops on a new position should be placed beforehand, too.

In the second case, for liquidation of one position and the opening of another position, a trailing stop can also be used along with the doubling size of the usual contract. After an order execution, a new position should be protected immediately by automatic stops.

CHAPTER 16

The Importance of Timing

The market has three basic characteristics that a trader must take into consideration: level, direction, and timing. Trading is the art of being in the right place at the right time, that is, on the right side of the market. I have already discussed how to determine the right place for entering the market and how to use the market fluctuations. Now, it's time to talk about the timing factor. As the market events develop (not only in space, but also in time), it is necessary to take into account the entire picture at any moment a position is opened or liquidated. Timing is an extremely important factor in trading, and a sense of timing is an essential component of a trader's success in the market. The right choice of timing for position opening and liquidation is a very complicated task and demands a lot of attention, patience, and (unfortunately) rather significant experience of a trader.

Thus, positions opened in the direction of particular market movement—at the moment when the market forms new high or low of the day—will give a trader some certain statistical advantage. This is especially true when the market simply doesn't have enough time to complete its average daily range within the period of time left before the end of a trading day.

Normally, it wouldn't be very difficult for an experienced technical trader to determine future market trading levels more or less precisely, but the forecast of the time frame of such an event is rather difficult if not impossible. Mistakes in precise forecasting are so great that they often compel a trader either to liquidate a potentially very promising position prematurely, or to keep a profitable position longer than necessary. An unprofitable position carried with a floating loss is often liquidated at the moment it has accumulated the greatest possible loss and right before a turn for the better.

133

However, the connection between amplitude of the market fluctuations and its direction also exists, and the knowledge of some common law related to timing could essentially help a trader in his choice of the right place at the right time. Besides, because the market is open 24 hours a day, it is quite natural that a trader is not capable of supervising it constantly. Hence, it is necessary to organize his working hours so that presence in the market would coincide with periods of the best activity and would bring a maximum possible effect. For these purposes, it is important to have an idea of how time and market space are tied together.

The market has to complete its average trading range daily. So, the distance between high and low of each next day can be projected in advance with certain accuracy.

This statement is one of the basic three postulates of my trading method. It is time to talk about it in more detail, because this fact has a direct relation to intraday speculative trade, and some of my trading templates are constructed on its basis.

Really, this feature of the market rather rigidly connects space and time. If you take into the account the inertia of the market, such an approach will allow you to more effectively determine the levels of opening and liquidating your positions, and to make these transactions at the right time.

Thus, the positions opened in the direction of the current market movement at the moment when the market forms new High or Low of the day will give traders some certain statistical advantage. This is especially true when the market simply doesn't have enough time to complete its average daily range within the period of time left before the end of a trading day.

To execute the order to open a new position, I typically use entry stops so as not to waste time on transaction execution while trying to place my order at a market price. Generally, such tactics works very well because, at the expense of stops accumulation, the market frequently accelerates at the moment of establishing a new daily High or Low.

This trading tactic is very effective when:

- Trading is made at a period of the best activity of the market.
- The currency chosen for trade has the largest average daily range.
- The position opens in a direction of the current intermediate trend.
- The establishment of new high or low coincides with a break of an important technical level.
- There is not enough time left until the end of the trading day, and the average minimum range typical for the given currency hasn't yet been formed.

The last item is especially interesting to traders, because it gives them a statistically advantageous position. The described situation hardly increases chances for taking profit, but at the same time allows the trader to calculate a point of the position liquidation. The position may be closed at the moment when the market achieves the average range in which it can liquidate your position, or it may be saved until the end of the day and be liquidated directly before closing of the market. In the second case, the intraday profit is frequently more significant, because the market often exceeds the minimum of its daytime range.

CYCLIC CHANGES IN MARKET ACTIVITY PERIODS

I have witnessed many similar cycles when, almost every day, not only USD/JPY but also USD/CHF, USD/DEM, and Cable formed their daily trading range during a single market session. Long-term supervision of the market has allowed me to determine some other laws having a direct relation to timing. These laws are considerably more important for a short-term trade than for a positional one. The intraday trade is most subject to influence of timing, and requires application of various trading tactics, depending on the moment of opening or liquidating a position.

From the start, I would like you to pay attention to the periodically varying character of market behavior. Activity of the market and an intraday trading range are not coordinated. Changes in market activity occur cyclically. They are characterized by displacement of periods of the increased and decreased activity on a 24-hour scale of a trading day during many consecutive days. For example, there have been cycles in which the daily trading range was completed in a period of one working session. For example, the daily range completion during the limited time is characterized by forming the top and bottom of the whole day during one of three basic sessions: Asian, European, or New York. It means that the high and low of the trading day were formed in no more than eight hours, and, for the rest of the trading day, the market was moving inside the already formed range.

Sometimes, these cycles are highly visible, and sometimes they are less obvious. Their variety is huge. From that great number of various cycles that I had to observe while trading the basic currencies, the following were the most memorable:

- The market formed its daily range during a single session. See Figures 16.1 a, b, and c.
- Directly before the New York session (10 to 20 minutes prior to its beginning), the market formed the top or bottom of the daily range. For example, within the time left until the end of the day, the market traded inside the already formed range. See Figure 16.2.

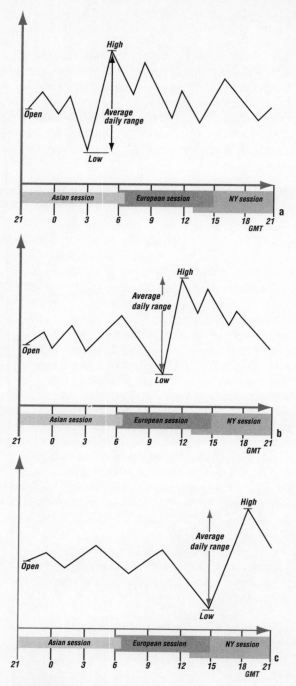

FIGURE 16.1 Single session market activity (a—Asian, b–European, c—North American).

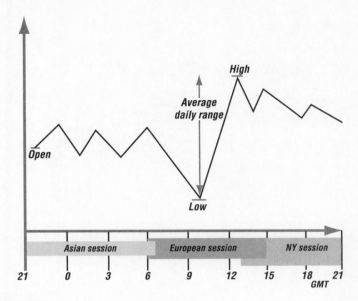

FIGURE 16.2

- The daily range activity was divided between sessions, and, during each session, the market expanded the previous range by $\frac{1}{3}$ the size of the daily range in one direction or the other. See Figure 16.3.
- The market completely formed its daily range by the end of the European trading session, and traded inside the already formed range for the rest of the day. See Figure 16.4.
- Within three hours before the end of the European session, the market almost doubled its trading range. See Figure 16.5.
- The market completely formed its daily range within three to four hours, and then traded only inside the already formed range. See Figure 16.6.
- The market increased its daily range significantly (40-60%) in an unusual time of the trading day, i.e., in a period between 3 to 5 P.M. NY time (8 to 10 P.M. GMT). See Figure 16.7.

These figures illustrate different market patterns in their relation to time matters. As you know, timing is a very important issue in the art of trading, and the ability to identify frequently changing behavioral market cycles can be helpful to a trader.

There were still a great number of other cycles of market activity, and all these possible variations cannot be listed. Because we can identify

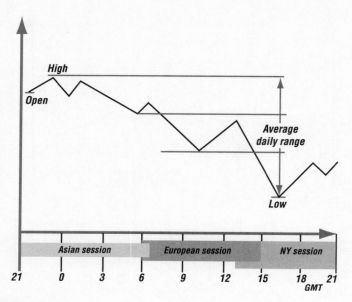

FIGURE 16.3

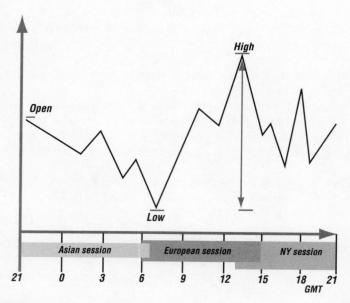

FIGURE 16.4

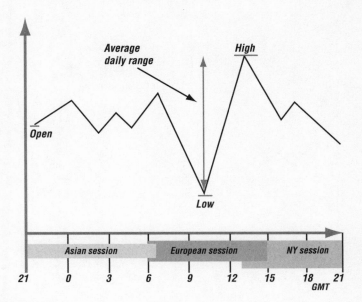

FIGURE 16.5

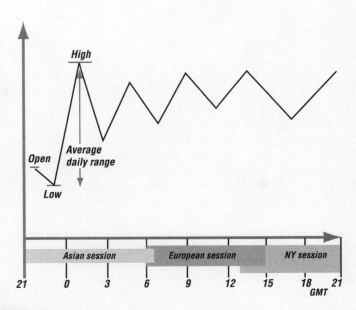

FIGURE 16.6

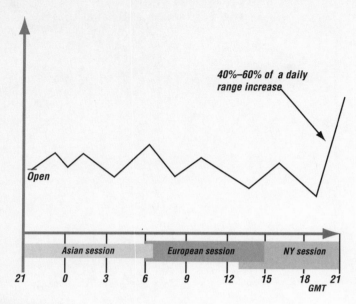

FIGURE 16.7

such cycles, we have a perfect opportunity to make a much more exact probability evaluation of the market movement during the following period of time in one direction or the other direction; and to reasonably plan a trader's time. As a trader discovers this regularity, it allows him to change the schedule of his presence in the market, avoiding periods of lowered activity and participating in high amplitude fluctuations. Some cyclic laws even allow you to trade automatically by placing preliminary stops and limits at certain established price levels.

Unfortunately, it is impossible to forecast the end of one cycle and the start of a new one, and also changes in market behavior. There could be many variations, and all of them can be characterized typically by one or several distinctive features. There are common periods of increased and decreased activity, and some similarity in a sequence of intraday fluctuations during all the cycles. Because such cycles basically last from several weeks to several months, the trader almost always has enough time not only to identify change in character of market behavior but also to use them in full measure for reception of the maximum profit. I try to reach the optimum trading results by selecting appropriate trading templates from my standard set and adjusting them to a current situation. The adjustment usually occurs at the moment of opening a new position on a timing scale inside one trading day.

CHAPTER 17

Trading Strategy During the Central Bank Intervention

From time to time, the central bank (CB) within a particular country, alone or with the support of the CBs of other countries, launches currency interventions into the market by buying up the weakening currency, in an attempt to artificially keep its rate stable. Bank of Japan (BoJ) is especially notable for such actions. It makes sudden and large-scale purchases of currency packages, thus keeping the yen rate against the dollar, or vice versa. This depends on the end of the currency channel acceptable for the CB at which the current rate is located. These actions of the CB always cause strong, fast, and large amplitude movement that may result in dramatic consequences for traders, leading to complete loss of their trading account. If traders are not ready for such action, this movement may inflict irreparable damage on their accounts within a few minutes.

To lower the risk of the loss during a sudden intervention and to use interventions for their benefit, traders should know and always remember the traits of this phenomenon, which is not rare in the currency market.

The first trait of an intervention is the direction of its movement. An intervention is always undertaken in the direction opposite to the main current trend. This can be seen in daily and weekly charts of currency rate fluctuations. See Figure 17.1.

The second trait is the amplitude of the movement. One should remember that an intervention is aimed at a significant correction of the present rates. This amplitude fluctuates from 300 to 600 pips, depending on the scale of the intervention and the number of its participants. During concerted interventions, when several CBs of different countries partici-

FIGURE 17.1 Every CB's intervention usually provides a very good opportunity to make a profitable trade with very little risk or even no risk at all. With a CB on your side, you can join its action and ride the market on its expense. Here you can see a chart that shows a huge day range caused by such an event.

pate in them, the amplitude is even greater. There are almost no cases in which the market returns to its pre-intervention levels during the same business day. It is also of great importance that, as a result of the intervention, even a minimum amplitude (300 to 350 pips) of the market rate fluctuation gives us an excellent opportunity to make a profitable transaction at almost no risk. See Figure 17.2.

The third trait, which is also favorable for the trader, is that rumors and information of a potential intervention appear on the market some time prior to real intervention. This helps the trader take necessary measures and get ready for such events.

Based on these traits, the trader should use the following strategy and tactics for the possible coming intervention:

Using the information that the present price level is unacceptable for certain CBs, you come to the conclusion that the market has entered the zone where the possibility of an intervention is high. From this moment on, at the beginning of each trading day, you place the trailing stop-loss order to open a new position at the distance of 70 to 100 pips from the current market price. You should do so on the assumption that, if the movement is fast, then your stop-loss order will work automatically and

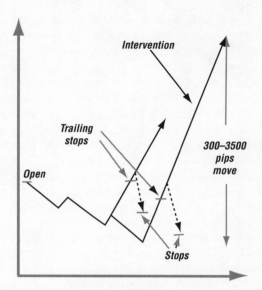

FIGURE 17.2 Trading strategy on concerted intervention.

much earlier than the market will make its minimum possible amplitude during the intervention.

Furthermore, watch the market behavior, because several different scenarios of the further development of the events are possible. If an intervention has not been launched but, for some reason, the market has turned back and is approaching your stop-loss order slowly, you should cancel your stop-loss order and transfer it farther, keeping the same distance of 70 to 100 pips from the current price. Slow movement of the market (even in the same direction from which the possible intervention is to be launched) is unacceptable, because my trailing stop-loss order was placed only on the expectation of the following event. If the position is triggered in the absence of the event I expected, my trailing stop-loss order is probably not going to work efficiently.

If the market continues its movement in the main trend, then in every 30 to 40 pips from its movement, you should place your trailing stop-loss order at the level that is closer to the current market price. (Here, it is essential to know that you should always begin by placing a new stop-loss order; and, only after that, cancel the old one so as not to miss the beginning of the intervention) Let us assume that fast and amplitude movement did take place. It passed through your stop-loss order and opened a new position for you automatically. Immediately after that, you should find the reason for this movement because it may be caused by reasons other than an intervention.

Sometimes such a movement may be caused by the market reaction to rumors that the CB, which is going to launch an intervention, is checking rates. This movement may also be the result of an extremely nervous market reaction to any other event, news or rumors. If an intervention has not been launched, you should square the open position that was taken, as soon as you find out that the surge of the market activity has not been caused by an intervention. You should do so, whether this position gives you a profit or a loss at the moment of its liquidation. If the information about the beginning of an intervention has been confirmed and by the moment you find out about it the market has passed less than 300 pips, you can strengthen the position. You can do it either at once or after the pullback of 50 to 70 pips from the maximum price level of the last movement.

When the market reaches the amplitude of movement of 300 to 400 pips as the consequence of the intervention, you can pocket the profit in full or partially. If the liquidation is partial, the trailing stop-loss order should be placed for the remaining part of the contract. You should place it not farther than the price level of the initial position, so that the profitable trade could not become its exact opposite.

Timely fixing of the profit should be done, as interventions are usually launched as extreme measures of correcting unfavorable market rates. In most cases, they are contrary to the objective circumstances of a fundamental nature. That is why the correction effect of an intervention often proves to be unstable. A few days after the intervention, the market may come back to the initial pre-intervention levels. Here, new danger of the CB's repeated actions might arise. You have to avoid the situation when a successfully opened position, which has been profitable from the very start, may become its extreme opposite. You have to avoid the loss of the greater part of the profit, as well. To attain this goal, you should fix your profit immediately after the market amplitude reaches 300 to 350 pips, or protect it by placing a trailing stop-loss order. Because most recent BoJ interventions were made just to prevent fast decline of the Japanese yen, the USD/JPY range is usually smaller than 300 to 350 pips; and you have to adjust your tactics accordingly, by having closer entry stops and taking quicker profits if you are not willing to take any chances.

PART V

Templates for Short-Term and Intraday Trading

The templates that I'm about to present you represent the systematic component of my discrete-systematic trading method. These templates were created to organize the trading process in the most effective, simple, and timesaving way, reduce stress, and save traders worry and money. Actual trading with use of the templates is based on recognition of certain market behavioral patterns.

To make a trade, you have to choose the correct template that corresponds with the current market outlook, and then follow the prescribed procedure automatically. Almost all of the templates can be customized to fit the needs of the majority of traders in terms of capital size and risk acceptance. Despite the fact that all the templates described here are divided into chapters devoted to different kinds of trading signals, the borderlines between templates from different categories are not so clear. Combinations composed by parts taken from two or more different templates can also be used. I believe that such an approach will eventually allow every trader to create his or her own individual and unique trading style and technique.

Start creating your own trading templates by using the basic ideas and principles described in the book and this particular part of it. As you understand, it was absolutely impossible to research and describe all possible options based on the ideas of this book, and turn them into different templates. Therefore, I have used only those basic ideas that should give you the ability to start making money from the very beginning. It has to give you a solid basis on which you can build your own trading style and technique, without risking too much and wasting money for testing something that may not even work properly.

Guide to Trade Templates:		
1. Potential profit and risks **evaluation marks scale:**	1. Very low	
	2. Low	
	3. Below average	
	4. Average	
	5. Above average	
	6. High	
	7. Very high	
2. Points to take profit (Target):	P1, P2, P3 etc.	
3. Profit/Loss (P/L) ratio estimation:	P>L	Positive
	P=L	Neutral
	P<L	Negative

CHAPTER 18

Average Daily Trading Range Templates

The markets have a strong tendency to complete their average trading range daily. Using this as a base, entry strategies can be employed, as described in the following templates. Please see Box 18.1 through Box 18.5, along with each box's corresponding figures.

Box 18.1			
Brief situation description:	From the day opening and throughout the Asian session, the market is drifting up and down on both sides from the opening price within a 30 to 50-pip range but without forming any specific pattern.		
Currency recommended for a trade:	USD/CHF, USD/JPY, EUR/USD, EUR/JPY and other Euro crosses.		
Trade characteristics:	Basic (conservative).		
Trade (entry point) suggestions:	Take a position in the direction of the move on the break of the opposite side of the range: **A. Buy** on the break of the previous range as soon as the market reaches the top and makes a new high directly after forming the bottom of the range, **OR** **B. Sell** on the break of the previous range as soon as the market reaches the bottom and makes a new low directly after forming the top of the range.		
Entry time:	The beginning of the European session, but not later than 2 to 3 hours into it.		
Entry execution:	Entry-stop or market order.		
Stop loss placed:	At the opposite side of the range. (Below the previous range low or above the previous range high.)		
Reverse if stops triggered:	Recommended with automatic entry stops.		
Target (custom choice):	30 to 40 pips **(P1)**	Average daily range **(P2)**	End of the day **(P3)**
Potential profit estimation:	30 to 100 pips		
Profit probability evaluation:	High		
Risk evaluation:	Low		
P/L ratio:	Negative to Positive		
Potential clues in favor of the open position:	The position was open in the direction of the most current medium-term trend. (In this case **P2** and **P3** schemes are preferable.)	The market has formed a flat surface on the opposite side of the range, where the stops are placed. This is a potential risk warning. Taking profit as soon as possible can solve the problem.	
Possible complications, disadvantages, and risk warnings, and advice to avoid them:	**RW:** The position was open against the direction of the most current medium-term trend.	**A:** Limit your profit with 30 to 40 pips or do not take a position at all.	
Additional notices, recommendations, and trading tips:	If the market did not give you the opportunity to pocket a profit or you did not take it for some other reason, then there is a high probability that, after the stops were triggered and position reversed, you will be able to cover the initial loss within the same trading day.		

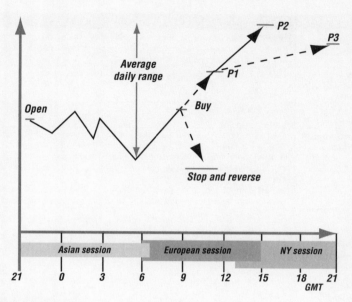

FIGURE 18.1a

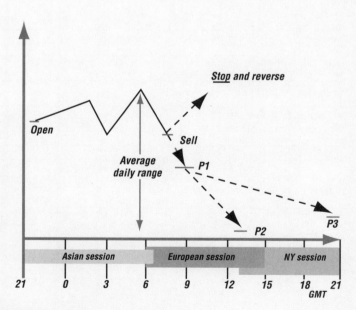

FIGURE 18.1b

Box 18.2

Brief situation description:	From the day opening during the Asian session, the market was drifting slowly in only one direction from the open price at a distance 40 to 60 pips without forming any specific pattern.
Currency recommended for a trade:	USD/CHF, USD/JPY, EUR/USD, EUR/JPY and other Euro crosses.
Trade characteristics:	Basic (conservative).
Trade (entry point) suggestions:	Take a position in the direction of the move on the break of the opposite side of the range: **A. Buy** on the break of the previous range as soon as the market reaches the top and makes a new high directly after forming the bottom of the range, **OR** **B. Sell** on the break of the previous range as soon as the market reaches the bottom and makes a new low directly after forming the top of the range.
Entry time:	European or NY session.
Entry execution:	Entry-stop order.
Stop loss placed: (Cannot be chosen in accordance with a trader's individual situation and preferences. Money management principles must apply.)	On the opposite side of the range. (Above the previous day high or below the previous day low.)
Reverse if stops triggered:	Recommended. (Automatic and simultaneous with stops.)
Target (custom choice):	Average daily range **(P1)** / End of the day **(P2)**
Potential profit estimation:	50 to 100 pips
Profit probability evaluation:	Average to High
Risk evaluation:	Average to Low
P/L ratio:	Neutral to Positive
Potential advantages in favor of the open position:	The position was open in the direction of the medium-term trend.	The position was open in the direction of the main move of the previous day.	The market broke an important trendline, support or resistance.
The most probable complications, disadvantages, and risk warnings, and advice to avoid them:	**RW#1:** The position was open against the direction of the medium-term trend. **RW#2:** The position was open against the main move of the previous day. **RW#3:** The market has formed a "flat surface" on the opposite side of the range.	**A#1:** Move your stops closer and place them above (below) the previous local extreme formed the same day. **A#2:** Same as above. **A#3:** Accept the risk.	

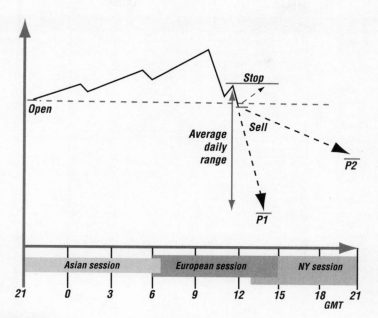

FIGURE 18.2a

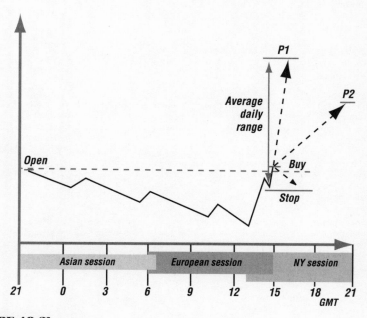

FIGURE 18.2b

Box 18.3

Brief situation description:	From the day opening during the Asian session, the market was drifting slowly in only one direction from the open price at a distance 40 to 60 pips without forming any specific pattern.
Currency recommended for a trade:	Cable, USD/CHF, USD/JPY, EUR/USD, EUR/JPY and other Euro crosses.
Trade characteristics:	Optional (risky).
Trade (entry point) suggestions:	Take a position in the opposite direction of the move and toward the open price of the day.
Entry time:	**A.** End of the Asian session—beginning of the European session; **OR** **B.** As soon as the range of 40 to 60 pips is formed, but not later than 2 to 3 hours into the European session.
Entry execution:	Market order.

Stop loss placed: (Can be chosen in accordance with a trader's individual situation and preferences. Money management principles must apply.)	50 pips from the position opening price.	Below the nearest obvious support or above the nearest resistance.	Above the previous day high (below the previous day low).	Behind the nearest major trendline (if applied).

Reverse if stops triggered:	Not recommended.

Target (custom choice):	The day open price **(P1)**	Average daily range **(P2)**	End of the day **(P3)**

Potential profit estimation:	50 to 160 pips
Profit probability evaluation:	Average to Above average
Risk evaluation:	Below average to Average
P/L ratio:	Neutral to Positive

Potential advantages in favor of the open position:	A flat surface on the opposite side of the range is formed.	Common gaps near the day open price are formed.	The main move of the previous day was in the same direction as your position is.

Possible complications, disadvantages, and risk warnings, and advice to avoid them:	**RW#1:** The position was open against the direction of the medium-term trend. **RW#2:** The position was open against the main move of the previous day.	**A#1:** Take profit at the day open price. **A#2:** Take profit at the day open price.

Additional notices, recommendations, and trading tips:	If the market after a position was open comes to the day open price, you can move your stops closer and place them right on the opposite side of the range. In this case, the target to take profit can also be moved further and placed at the end of the day or at average day range.

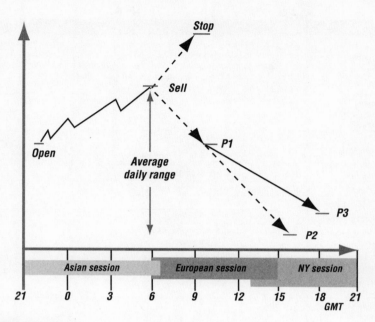

FIGURE 18.3a

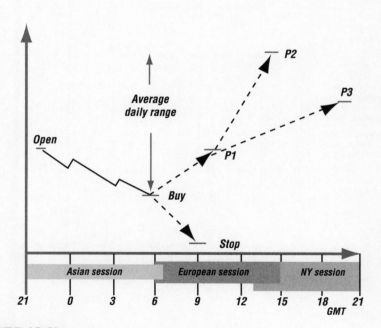

FIGURE 18.3b

Box 18.4

Brief situation description:	The market has formed the day range 80 to 100 pips by the end of the European session—beginning of the NY session. Now it's closer to the end of the range, which is opposite to the previous day's main move direction (or the medium-term trend direction) after going all the way from the opposite side of the range.
Currency recommended for a trade:	USD/CHF, USD/JPY, Cable, EUR/USD, EUR/JPY and other Euro crosses.
Trade characteristics:	Trade of opportunity.
Trade (entry point) suggestions:	Open a position in the direction of the main move of the previous day (or the medium-term trend) at 30 pips ahead of the day high or low.
Entry time:	Very late European session and/or NY session.
Entry execution:	Entry-stop order.
Stop loss placed:	At the closest side of the range.
Reverse if stops triggered:	Recommended with automatic entry-stops.
Target (custom choice):	Average daily range **(P1)** / End of the day **(P2)**
Potential profit estimation:	100 to 140 pips
Profit probability evaluation:	Average
Risk evaluation:	Below average
P/L ratio:	Positive
Potential advantages in favor of the open position:	N/A
Possible complications, disadvantages, and risk warnings, and advice to avoid them:	N/A
Additional notices, recommendations, and trading tips:	If the stops were triggered before the profit is taken, there is a good probability to cover the initial loss within the same trading day.

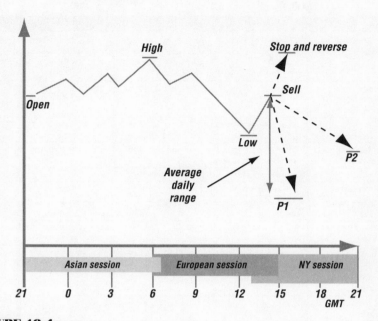

FIGURE 18.4a

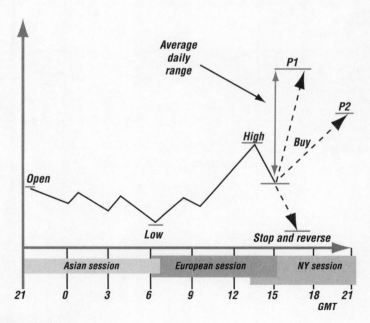

FIGURE 18.4b

Box 18.5	
Brief situation description:	The market makes a new intraday high or low after going all the way from the opposite side of the intraday range. At this moment the range is $^2/_3$ or more of the size of an average daily range. Just 3 to 5 hours or less are left till the end of the trading day.
Currency recommended for a trade:	USD/CHF, EUR/USD, EUR/JPY and other Euro crosses.
Trade characteristics:	Basic (conservative).
Trade (entry point) suggestions:	Enter a position in the direction of the move on the break of the previous intraday high or low.
Entry time:	Late NY session.
Entry execution:	Entry-stop order.

Stop loss placed:	On the other side of the previous range.	On the previous intraday swing top/bottom.
Reverse if stops triggered:	Recommended with automatic entry-stop.	Cautiously recommended.

Target (custom choice):	Average daily range **(P1)**	End of the day **(P2)**	Major trendline, support or resistance **(P3)**
Potential profit estimation:	30 to 60 pips		
Profit probability evaluation:	Very high		
Risks evaluation:	Very low		
P/L ratio:	Negative		
Potential advantages in favor of the open position:	N/A		
Possible complications, disadvantages, and risk warnings, and solutions to avoid them:	N/A		
Additional notices, recommendations, and trading tips:	N/A		

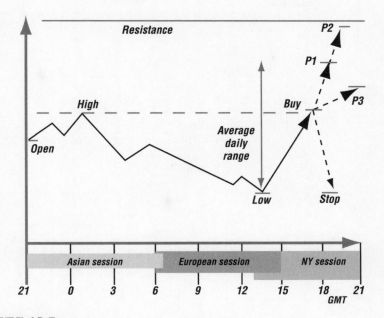

FIGURE 18.5a

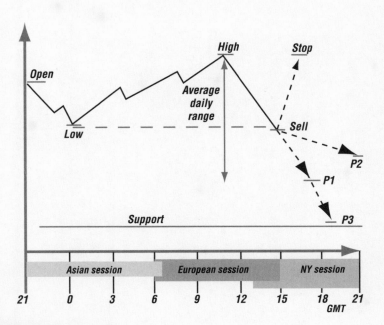

FIGURE 18.5b

CHAPTER 19

Technical Formation Templates

C ommon technical formations such as channels, triangles, diamonds, head and shoulders, and double tops and bottoms provide trade entry possibilities as described in the following templates. Please see Box 19.1 through Box 19.15, along with each box's accompanying figures.

Box 19.1

Brief situation description:	At the beginning of the day during the Asian session, the market has formed a narrow (20 to 30-pip) comb-like horizontal channel. Then a break on one side occurred.		
Currency recommended for a trade:	All majors and crosses.		
Trade characteristics:	Basic (conservative).		
Trade (entry point) suggestions:	Ignore the first break of one of the sides and enter the market on the break of the second side of the channel. The position has to be taken in the direction of the move.		
Entry time:	Asian or early European sessions.		
Entry execution:	Entry-stop order.		
Stop loss placed:	At the other side of the previous intraday range.		
Reverse if stops triggered:	Recommended automatic entry-stop order.		
Target (custom choice):	30 to 40 pips **(P1)**	Average daily range **(P2)**	End of the day **(P3)**
Potential profit estimation:	30 to 120 pips		
Profit probability evaluation:	Very high		
Risks evaluation:	Very low		
P/L ratio:	Neutral to Positive		
Potential advantages in favor of the open position:	The position was open in the direction of the current medium-term trend.		
Possible complications, disadvantages, and risk warnings, and solutions to avoid them:	**RW:** The position was open against the direction of the current medium-term trend.		**A:** Take profit in accordance with Target 1.
Additional notices, recommendations, and trading tips:	N/A		

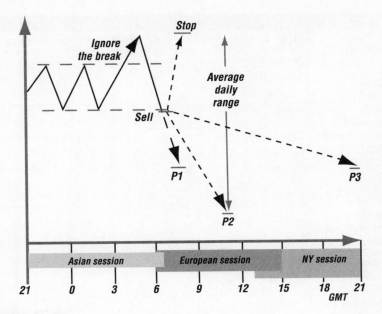

FIGURE 19.1a

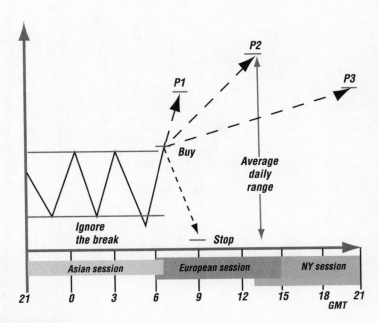

FIGURE 19.1b

Box 19.2	
Brief situation description:	At the beginning of the day during the Asian session, the market has formed a narrow (20 to 30-pip) comb-like horizontal channel. It usually can be identified on 5 to 10-min charts.
Currency recommended for a trade:	USD/CHF, USD/JPY, Cable, EUR/USD, EUR/JPY and other Euro crosses.
Trade characteristics:	Optional (risky).
Trade (entry point) suggestions:	Take a position on the first break of either side in the direction of the move.
Entry time:	Asian session.
Entry execution:	Entry-stop order.
Stop loss placed:	At the opposite side of the channel.
Reverse if stops triggered:	Recommended (automatic entry-stops order).
Target (NO custom choice):	20 to 30 pips
Potential profit estimation:	20 to 30 pips
Profit probability evaluation:	Average
Risks evaluation:	Average
P/L ratio:	Negative
Potential advantages in favor of the open position:	N/A
Possible complications, disadvantages, and risk warnings, and solutions to avoid them:	Such a trade requires a very precise execution that can be achieved with a good dealer or broker company. It also can be recommended for experienced traders only.
Additional notices, recommendations, and trading tips:	I recommend this particular trade only because the risk taken is very small. Also, a trader usually has enough time to pocket a small profit in this trade. The reverse (if the stops were triggered) most likely will cover the initial loss soon enough. However, in some relatively rare cases, an unexpected and fast move may happen. It can provide a profit that is much bigger than the projected target shown in this table. (Not a good choice for a conservative trader, though.)

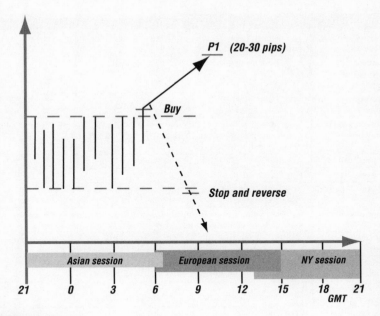

FIGURE 19.2a

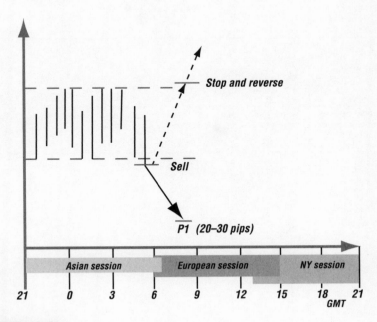

FIGURE 19.2b

Box 19.3			
Brief situation description:	The market has formed a horizontal channel, which can be identified on hourly and daily charts.		
Currency recommended for a trade:	All majors and crosses.		
Trade characteristics:	Basic (conservative).		
Trade (entry point) suggestions:	Ignore the first break of one of the sides and enter the market on the break of the second side of the channel. The position has to be taken in the direction of the move.		
Entry time:	Any time.		
Entry execution:	Entry-stop order.		
Stop loss placed:	At the other side of the current day range.	20 to 30 pips below the broken line.	Other
Reverse if stops triggered:	Recommended automatic entry-stop order in accordance with money management individual requirements and technical market picture.		
Target (custom choice):	Average daily range **(P1)**	End of the day **(P2)**	Width of the channel **(P3)** — Other
Potential profit estimation:	N/A		
Profit probability evaluation:	Very high		
Risks evaluation:	Very low		
P/L ratio:	Positive		
Potential advantages in favor of the open position:	The position was open in the direction of the current medium-term trend.		
Possible complications, disadvantages, and risk warnings, and solutions to avoid them:	N/A		
Additional notices, recommendations, and trading tips:	Such a trade can also be turned into longer-term position with technical targets located outside of one-day trading range.		

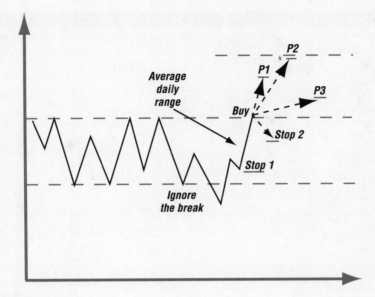

FIGURE 19.3a

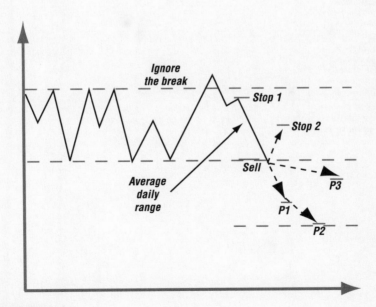

FIGURE 19.3b

Box 19.4

Brief situation description:	The market has formed a horizontal channel, which can be identified on hourly and daily charts.
Currency recommended for a trade:	All majors and crosses.
Trade characteristics:	Basic (conservative).
Trade (entry point) suggestions:	Enter the first break of one of the sides. The position has to be taken in the direction of the move.
Entry time:	Any time.
Entry execution:	Entry-stop order.
Stop loss placed:	At the other side of the previous intraday range.
Reverse if stops triggered:	Recommended (automatic entry-stop order).

Target (custom choice):	Average daily range **(P1)**	End of the day **(P2)**	Width of the channel **(P3)**	Other
Potential profit estimation:	N/A			
Profit probability evaluation:	High			
Risks evaluation:	Low			
P/L ratio:	Positive			

Potential advantages in favor of the open position:	The position was open in the direction of the current medium-term trend.	
Possible complications, disadvantages, and risk warnings, and solutions to avoid them:	**RW:** The position was open against the direction of the current medium-term trend.	**A:** Accept the risk.
Additional notices, recommendations, and trading tips:	Such a trade can also be turned into a longer-term position with technical targets located outside of a one-day trading range.	

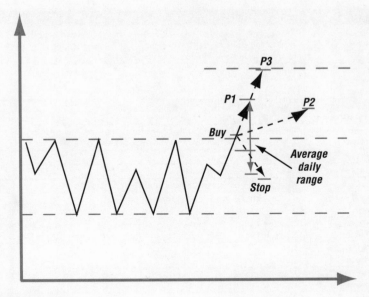

FIGURE 19.4a

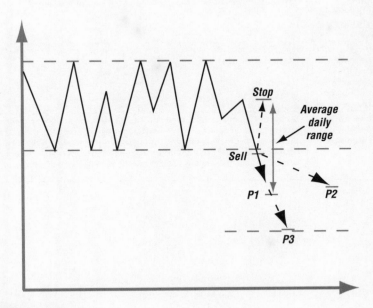

FIGURE 19.4b

Box 19.5

Brief situation description:	The market has formed a horizontal channel, which can be identified on hourly and daily charts. There were at least three touches on one side of a channel and two on the opposite.
Currency recommended for a trade:	All majors and crosses.
Trade characteristics:	Trade of opportunity.
Trade (entry point) suggestions:	Enter the market on the third approach to the side. The position has to be taken in the direction towards the opposite side of a channel.
Entry time:	Any time.
Entry execution:	Limit order or market order.
Stop loss placed:	Right behind the closest border of the channel (15 to 25 pips).
Reverse if stops triggered:	Recommended (automatic entry-stop order).

Target (custom choice):	Average daily range **(P1)**	End of the day **(P2)**	The opposite side of the channel **(P3)**	Other technical level inside the channel
Potential profit estimation:	N/A			
Profit probability evaluation:	Above average			
Risks evaluation:	Below average			
P/L ratio:	Positive			

Potential advantages in favor of the open position:	The position was open in the direction of the current medium-term trend.	
Possible complications, disadvantages, and risk warnings, and solutions to avoid them:	**RW:** The position was open against the direction of the current medium-term trend.	**A:** Accept the risk.
Additional notices, recommendations, and trading tips:	Such a trade can also be turned into a longer-term position with technical targets located outside of a one-day trading range. Especially if the position is open in the direction of a current longer-term trend and, in this case, a trader can wait and see if the other side of the channel will be broken or not. (A break usually follows soon after the **fourth** touch of a line.)	

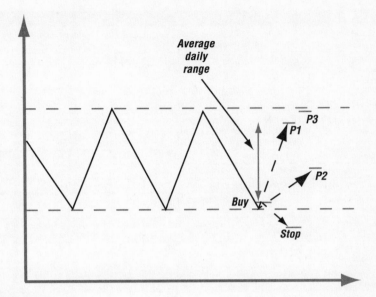

FIGURE 19.5a

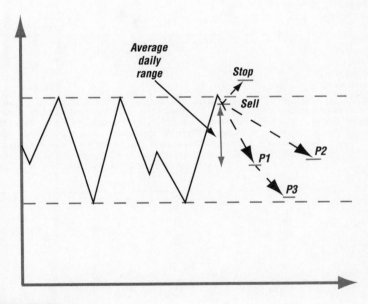

FIGURE 19.5b

Box 19.6				
Brief situation description:	The market has formed an inclined channel, which can be identified on hourly and daily charts.			
Currency recommended for a trade:	All majors and crosses.			
Trade characteristics:	Basic (conservative).			
Trade (entry point) suggestions:	Enter the market at the **lower** border of an **ascending** channel or at the **upper** border of a **descending** one. The position is taken in the direction towards the opposite side of a channel.			
Entry time:	Any time.			
Entry execution:	Limit order or market order.			
Stop loss placed:	Right behind the closest border of the channel (10 to 20 pips).			
Reverse if stops triggered:	Recommended (automatic entry-stop order).			
Target (custom choice):	Average daily range **(P1)**	End of the day **(P2)**	The opposite side of the channel **(P3)**	Other technical level inside the channel
Potential profit estimation:	N/A			
Profit probability evaluation:	Above average			
Risks evaluation:	Below average			
P/L ratio:	Positive			
Potential advantages in favor of the open position:	N/A			
Possible complications, disadvantages, and risk warnings, and solutions to avoid them:	N/A			
Additional notices, recommendations, and trading tips:	Such a trade can also be turned into a longer-term position with technical targets located outside of a one-day trading range when it is open in the direction of a current longer-term trend. (Be careful, because a break usually follows soon after the **fourth** touch of a line.) If the stops were triggered, then it is possible that the initial loss will be covered very soon after the actual break of the borderline. A position reverse may turn into a trade based on Box 19.5.			

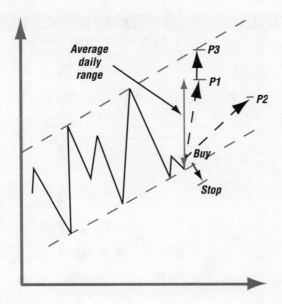

FIGURE 19.6a

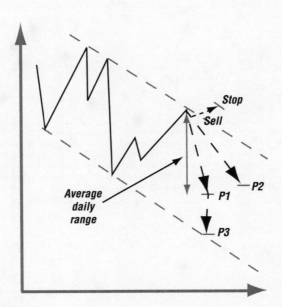

FIGURE 19.6b

Box 19.7				
Brief situation description:	The market has formed an inclined channel, which can be identified on hourly and daily charts.			
Currency recommended for a trade:	All majors and crosses.			
Trade characteristics:	Optional.			
Trade (entry point) suggestions:	Enter the market on the approach to the **lower** side of a **descending** channel or at the **upper** border of an **ascending** one. (The position is taken in the direction towards the opposite side of a channel.)			
Entry time:	Any time.			
Entry execution:	Limit order or market order.			
Stop loss placed:	Right behind the closest border of the channel (10 to 20 pips).			
Reverse if stops triggered:	Not recommended (if no other technical reason present).			
Target (custom choice):	Average daily range **(P1)**	End of the day **(P2)**	The opposite side of the channel **(P3)**	Other technical level inside the channel
Potential profit estimation:	N/A			
Profit probability evaluation:	Average			
Risks evaluation:	Average			
P/L ratio:	Positive			
Potential advantages in favor of the open position:	N/A			
Possible complications, disadvantages, and risk warnings, and solutions to avoid them:	N/A			
Additional notices, recommendations, and trading tips:	Such a trade usually cannot be turned into a longer-term position with technical targets located outside of a one-day trading range. Usually the true reverse can be expected if the market fails to reach the support of a descending channel or a resistance of an ascending one. So the trade described in this template is a counter trade against the current trend, and the profit better be taken as soon as possible.			

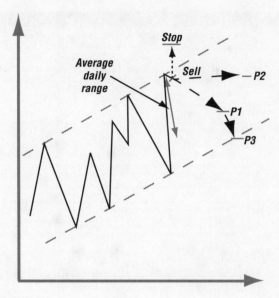

FIGURE 19.7a

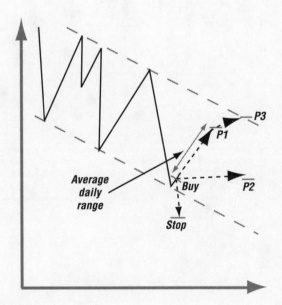

FIGURE 19.7b

Box 19.8			
Brief situation description:	The market has formed an inclined channel, which can be identified on hourly and daily charts. This trade would be the continuation of the one described in Box 19.6 (in case the stops were triggered and the position reversed). It can also be traded independently, and the signal to enter the market would be the break of the border of such a channel.		
Currency recommended for a trade:	All majors and crosses.		
Trade characteristics:	Basic (conservative).		
Trade (entry point) suggestions:	Enter the market on the break of the **lower** side of an **ascending** channel or at the **upper** border of a **descending** one.		
Entry time:	Any time.		
Entry execution:	Entry-stop order.		
Stop loss placed:	The opposite side of the current day range (if close enough).	Other technical level inside the current day range.	
Reverse if stops triggered:	Recommended (automatic entry-stop order) at the opposite side of a current day range.		
Target (custom choice):	Average daily range **(P1)**	End of the day **(P2)**	Other
Potential profit estimation:	N/A		
Profit probability evaluation:	High		
Risks evaluation:	Low		
P/L ratio:	Neutral to Positive		
Potential advantages in favor of the open position:	N/A		
Possible complications, disadvantages, and risk warnings, and solutions to avoid them:	N/A		
Additional notices, recommendations, and trading tips:	Such a trade can also be turned into a longer-term position with technical targets located outside the day-trading range. In this case, the position was open following a signal indicating potential trend change, and might be kept for longer term.		

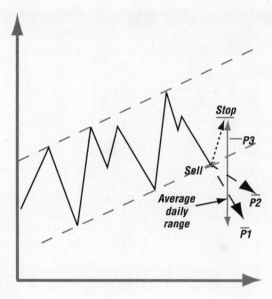

FIGURE 19.8a

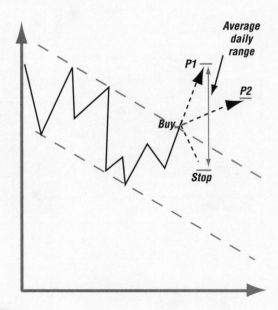

FIGURE 19.8b

Box 19.9

Brief situation description:	The market has formed a triangle, which can be identified on intraday or daily charts.			
Currency recommended for a trade:	All majors and crosses.			
Trade characteristics:	Basic (conservative).			
Trade (entry point) suggestions:	Enter the market on the break of either side of a triangle.			
Entry time:	Any time.			
Entry execution:	Entry-stop order.			
Stop loss placed:	The opposite side of the triangle (if it is narrow enough).	The opposite side of the current day range (if close enough).	Other technical level inside the current day ranges (if choice #2 is outside the acceptable risk level).	Other.
Reverse if stops triggered:	Recommended (automatic entry-stop order) in cases 1 and 2.			
Target (custom choice):	Average daily range (**P1**)	End of the day (**P2**)	Other	
Potential profit estimation:	N/A			
Profit probability evaluation:	High			
Risks evaluation:	Low			
P/L ratio:	Neutral to Positive			
Potential advantages in favor of the open position:	This trade is easy to plan in advance, because there is always enough time to identify the triangle and to make a sufficient trading plan. Also, the false break is mostly as good as a true one and indicates the market's intention to choose the opposite direction for the next move, which is also important for planning of the next trade.			
Possible complications, disadvantages, and risk warnings, and solutions to avoid them:	N/A			
Additional notices, recommendations, and trading tips:	It should be remembered that usually a break follows a fourth touch of a triangle's borderline. Such a trade can be turned into a longer-term position with technical targets located outside of the day trading range if a particular triangle is big enough.			

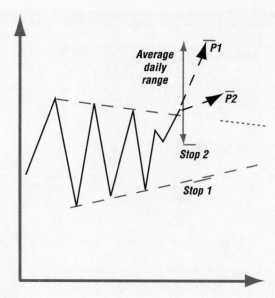

FIGURE 19.9a

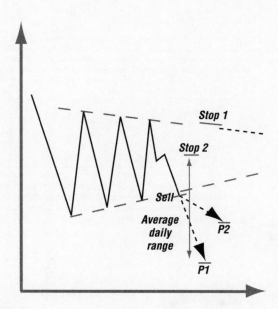

FIGURE 19.9b

Box 19.10

Brief situation description:	The market is forming a potential triangle, which can be identified on hourly or daily charts. Such a conclusion can be made only after the market has already formed one of the sides of the triangle completely. *Completely* means that one borderline of such a formation can be drawn through three or more significant points (highs or lows). It also has two significant points on the other side, which allow us to guess that the pattern we can see now will become a triangle in the near future.
Currency recommended for a trade:	All majors and crosses.
Trade characteristics:	Trade of opportunity.
Trade (entry point) suggestions:	Enter the market at the projected point, where the third touch of the second side of the triangle takes place. The position should be open in the direction of the opposite side of the formation.
Entry time:	Any time.
Entry execution:	Limit or market order.
Stop loss placed:	20 pips behind the nearest borderline, which is forming a triangle.
Reverse if stops triggered:	Recommended (automatic entry-stop order).

Target (custom choice):	Average daily range **(P1)**	End of the day **(P2)**	The opposite side of a triangle **(P3)**
Potential profit estimation:	N/A		
Profit probability evaluation:	Average		
Risks evaluation:	Average		
P/L ratio:	Positive		
Potential advantages in favor of the open position:	This trade is easy to plan in advance, because there should be enough time to identify a triangle even while it is still in the forming process.		
Possible complications, disadvantages, and risk warnings, and solutions to avoid them:	N/A		
Additional notices, recommendations, and trading tips:	In case the stops are triggered and the position was reversed, the initial loss most likely will be covered soon enough. It should also be remembered that usually a break follows a fourth touch of a triangle's borderline. Such a trade can be turned into a longer-term position with technical targets located outside of the day trading range if a particular triangle is big enough.		

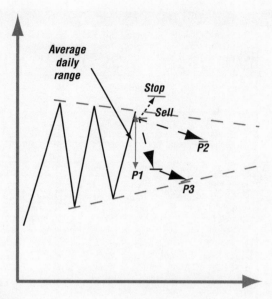

FIGURE 19.10a

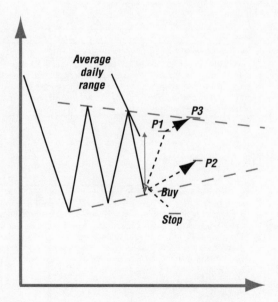

FIGURE 19.10b

Box 19.11

Brief situation description:	The market has formed a diamond, which can be identified on intraday or daily charts. Because the diamond can be considered as two triangles merged together, the recommendations are basically the same as in the case of a regular triangle. See Box 19.9.
Currency recommended for a trade:	All majors and crosses.
Trade characteristics:	Basic (conservative).
Trade (entry point) suggestions:	Enter the market on the break of either side of a diamond.
Entry time:	Any time.
Entry execution:	Entry-stop order.

Stop loss placed:	The opposite side of the triangle (if it is narrow enough).	The opposite side of the current day range (if close enough).	Other technical level inside the current day ranges (if choice #2 is outside the acceptable risk level).	Other

Reverse if stops triggered:	Recommended (automatic entry-stop order) in cases 1 and 2.

Target (custom choice):	Average daily range **(P1)**	End of the day **(P2)**	Other

Potential profit estimation:	N/A
Profit probability evaluation:	High
Risks evaluation:	Low
P/L ratio:	Neutral to Positive
Potential advantages in favor of the open position:	This trade is easy to plan in advance, since there is always enough time to identify the triangle and to make a sufficient trading plan. Also, the false break is mostly as good as a true one and indicates the market's intention to choose the opposite direction for the next move, which is also important for planning of the next trade.
Possible complications, disadvantages, and risk warnings, and solutions to avoid them:	N/A
Additional notices, recommendations, and trading tips:	A diamond is a rare formation. The first half of it could be a real disaster for a trader, because it represents a broadening triangle that is very difficult to identify before it is fully formed and very difficult to trade on. The rest is much easier, and no particular problem with trading on diamond should arise. It has to be remembered that usually a break follows a fourth touch of diamond's second half borderline. Such a trade can be turned into a longer-term position with technical targets located outside the day trading range, if a particular diamond is big enough.

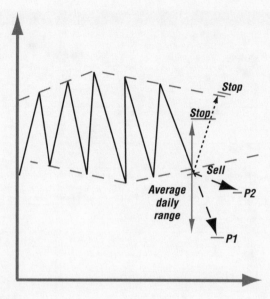

FIGURE 19.11a

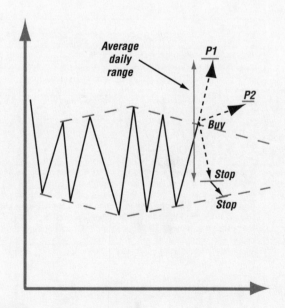

FIGURE 19.11b

Box 19.12			
Brief situation description:	The market is forming a potential diamond formation, which can be identified on hourly or daily charts. Such a conclusion can be made only after the market has already formed the left side of the formation (which is nothing but a broadening triangle) and at the moment is forming a second half of the formation. The second half is also a triangle, but a regular one. So, the recommendations for a trade are pretty much the same as in the case of a regular triangle.		
Currency recommended for a trade:	All majors and crosses.		
Trade characteristics:	Trade of opportunity.		
Trade (entry point) suggestions:	Enter the market at the projected point where the third touch of the second side of the triangle (second diamond part) takes place. The position should be open in the direction towards the opposite side of the formation.		
Entry time:	Any time.		
Entry execution:	Limit or market order.		
Stop loss placed:	20 pips behind the nearest borderline, which is forming a triangle.		
Reverse if stops triggered:	Recommended (automatic entry-stop order).		
Target (custom choice):	Average daily range **(P1)**	End of the day **(P2)**	The opposite side of a diamond **(P3)**
Potential profit estimation:	N/A		
Profit probability evaluation:	Average		
Risks evaluation:	Average		
P/L ratio:	Positive		
Potential advantages in favor of the open position:	This trade is easy to plan in advance, because there should be enough time to identify a triangle even while it is still in the forming process.		
Possible complications, disadvantages, and risk warnings, and solutions to avoid them:	N/A		
Additional notices, recommendations, and trading tips:	In case the stops are triggered and the position was reversed, the initial loss most likely will be covered soon enough. Remember that usually a break follows a fourth touch of a triangle's borderline. Such a trade can be turned into a longer-term position with technical targets located outside of the day trading range, if a particular triangle is big enough.		

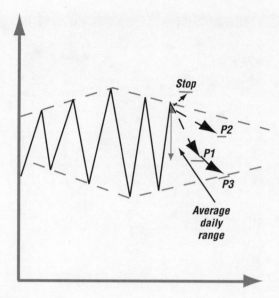

FIGURE 19.12a

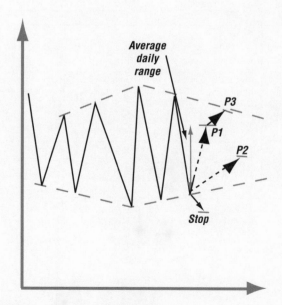

FIGURE 19.12b

Box 19.13

Brief situation description:	The market is forming a potential head and shoulders formation (inverted H&S formation as well) on hourly or daily charts, which cannot be identified as such since it is only a projection at the moment. The projection can be made at the moment when the market has already formed what may appear to be the left shoulder, the head, and the first half of the right shoulder. It works best when seen on hourly and daily charts.
Currency recommended for a trade:	All majors and crosses.
Trade characteristics:	Trade of opportunity.
Trade (entry point) suggestions:	Enter the market at the projected point where the projected top (bottom) of the second shoulder could be formed.
Entry time:	Any time.
Entry execution:	Limit or market order.
Stop loss placed:	Depends on the time frame and the scale of the potential formation. The trailing stop can also be used if some floating profit accumulated.
Reverse if stops triggered:	Not recommended.
Target:	Measured objective **(P1)**
Potential profit estimation:	N/A
Profit probability evaluation:	Below average
Risks evaluation:	Above average
P/L ratio:	Positive
Potential advantages in favor of the open position:	N/A
Possible complications, disadvantages, and risk warnings, and solutions to avoid them:	This trade is not easy to plan in advance. A good imagination should help, but, from the other side, it can be excessive too. The trade also requires a lot of practical experience from a trader.
Additional notices, recommendations, and trading tips:	In case of a successful entry, the profit is usually very significant, especially to enter the position on a bigger scale. It is better for longer-term positional trading rather than for intraday.

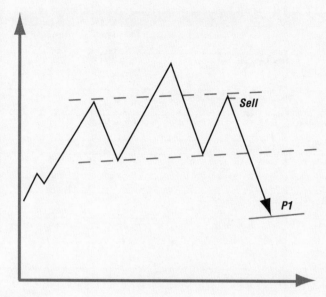

FIGURE 19.13a

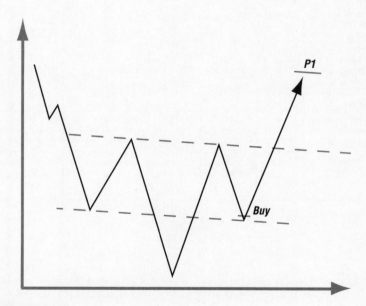

FIGURE 19.13b

Box 19.14

Brief situation description:	A head and shoulders formation (inverted H&S formation as well) is fully formed on hourly or daily charts.
Currency recommended for a trade:	All majors and crosses.
Trade characteristics:	Classic (textbook style).
Trade (entry point) suggestions:	Enter the market on the break of the neckline.
Entry time:	Any time.
Entry execution:	Entry-stop order.

Stop loss placed:	The opposite side of the day range.	Above (below) the top (bottom) of the right shoulder.

Reverse if stops triggered:	Recommended.

Target:	Measured objective (P1)	End of the day (P2)	Average daily range (P3)	Other

Potential profit estimation:	N/A
Profit probability evaluation:	Average
Risks evaluation:	Average
P/L ratio:	Positive
Potential advantages in favor of the open position:	N/A
Possible complications, disadvantages, and risk warnings, and solutions to avoid them:	N/A
Additional notices, recommendations, and trading tips:	Although this formation is classic (that means it is widely known and easily recognizable), the chance that the market will behave exactly the way as it is described in technical analysis textbooks is questionable. I do not usually trade on it without having some other reasons to enter a position at the break of a neckline of H&S. However, sometimes it works and, therefore, cannot be ignored completely. Usually the harder the identification, the better it works.

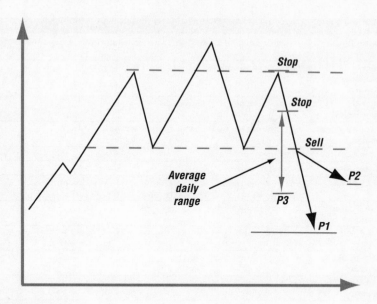

FIGURE 19.14a

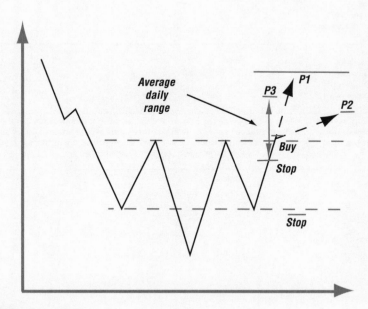

FIGURE 19.14b

Box 19.15

Brief situation description:	A double (triple) top (bottom) formation is fully formed on hourly or daily charts.		
Currency recommended for a trade:	All majors and crosses.		
Trade characteristics:	Classic (textbook recommended).		
Trade (entry point) suggestions:	Enter the market on the break of the neckline.		
Entry time:	Any time.		
Entry execution:	Entry-stop order.		
Stop loss placed:	The opposite side of the day range	Above (below) the line drawn through both tops (bottoms)	Other
Reverse if stops triggered:	Recommended		
Target:	Measured objective **(P1)**	End of the day **(P2)**	Average daily range **(P3)**	Other
Potential profit estimation:	N/A		
Profit probability evaluation:	Below average		
Risks evaluation:	Above average		
P/L ratio:	Positive		
Potential advantages in favor of the open position:	N/A		
Possible complications, disadvantages, and risk warnings, and solutions to avoid them:	N/A		
Additional notices, recommendations, and trading tips:	Same thing as with the H&S formation. This formation is also a classic one, but the chance to see the exact behavioral pattern prescribed by technical analysis textbooks is slim. I do not usually trade on it without having some other reasons to enter a position at the neckline break.		

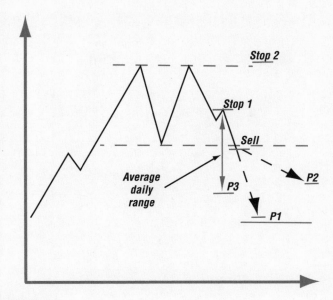

FIGURE 19.15a

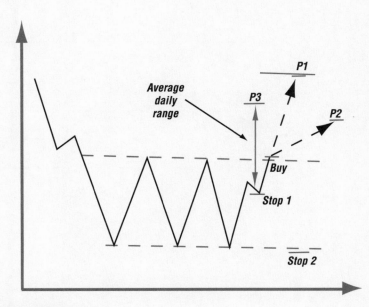

FIGURE 19.15b

CHAPTER 20

Trendlines, Support, and Resistance Templates

The following templates are based on trendlines, supports, and resistances. Please see Box 20.1 through Box 20.7, along with each box's accompanying figures.

Box 20.1

Brief situation description:	The market has formed on daily charts a specific formation, which I call a comb. (This is a sort of short-term trend seen on frame charts any time including intraday, daily, and weekly.)
Currency recommended for a trade:	USD/CHF, USD/JPY, EUR/USD, EUR/JPY and other Euro crosses.
Trade characteristics:	Basic (conservative).
Trade (entry point) suggestions:	Take a position in the direction of the move on the break of the trendline limiting a comb from one side: **A. Buy** on the break of the descending line, **OR** **B. Sell** on the break of the ascending line.
Entry time:	Any time.
Entry execution:	Entry-stop order.
Stop-loss placed: (Cannot be chosen in accordance with a trader's individual situation and preferences. Money management principles must apply.)	On the opposite side of the current day range. (Above the previous day high or below the previous day low.)
Reverse if stops triggered:	Recommended. (Automatic and simultaneous with stops.)

Target (custom choice):	Average daily range **(P1)**	End of the day **(P2)**	Other
Potential profit estimation:	N/A		
Profit probability evaluation:	Average to High		
Risks evaluation:	Average to Low		
P/L ratio:	Positive		
Potential advantages in favor of the open position:	The position was open in the direction of the medium-term trend.	The position was open in the direction of the main move of the previous day.	
The most probable complications, disadvantages, and risk warnings, and advice to avoid them:	**RW#1:** The position was open against the direction of the medium-term trend. **RW#2:** The position was open against the main move of the previous day.	**A#1:** Move your stops closer and place them above (below) the previous local extreme formed the same day. **A#2:** Same as above.	

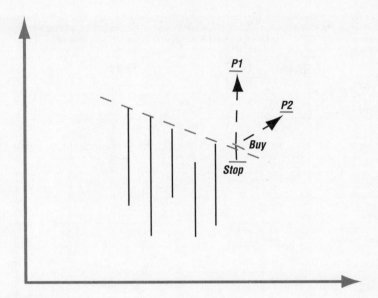

FIGURE 20.1a

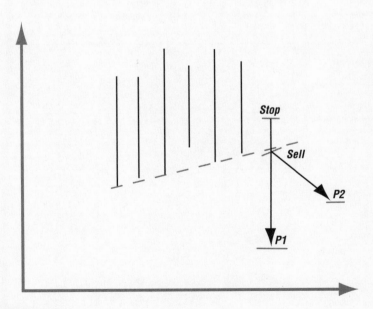

FIGURE 20.1b

Box 20.2

Brief situation description:	The market has formed on intraday charts a comb formation.		
Currency recommended for a trade:	USD/CHF, USD/JPY and some EUR crosses.		
Trade characteristics:	Optional (risky).		
Trade (entry point) suggestions:	Enter the market on the break of the line.		
Entry time:	Any time.		
Entry execution:	Entry-stop order.		
Stop loss placed:	The opposite side of the day range	The nearest technical level	Other
Reverse if stops triggered:	Recommended.		
Target (depends on the time frame):	End of the day **(P1)**	Average daily range **(P2)**	Other
Potential profit estimation:	N/A		
Profit probability evaluation:	Average		
Risks evaluation:	Average		
P/L ratio:	Neutral		
Potential advantages in favor of the open position:	**A.** The position was open in the direction of the main move of the day. **B.** The break of the line occurred simultaneously with forming of the new low or new high of the day.		
Possible complications, disadvantages, and risk warnings, and solutions to avoid them:	N/A		
Additional notices, recommendations, and trading tips:	To trade combs on an intraday basis is a bit problematic. It is better to trade having some other technical reasons to enter a position, because trading in limited time and space is always difficult for a trader. However, sometimes it works extremely well if you take profit at the right time.		

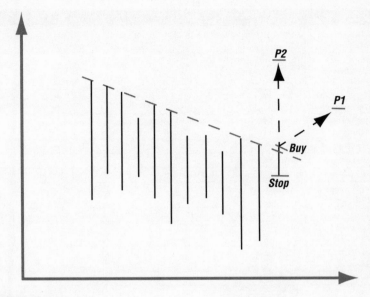

FIGURE 20.2a

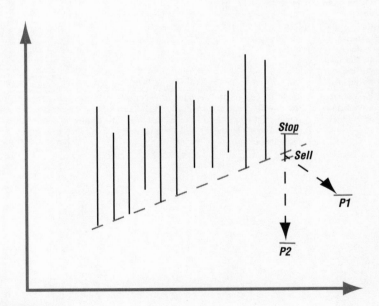

FIGURE 20.2b

Box 20.3			
Brief situation description:	A flat surface is formed on daily charts.		
Currency recommended for a trade:	All majors and crosses.		
Trade characteristics:	Optional.		
Trade (entry point) suggestions:	Enter the market on the break of the surface.		
Entry time:	Any time.		
Entry execution:	Entry-stop order.		
Stop loss placed:	The opposite side of the day range	Other technical level	
Reverse if stops triggered:	Possible.		
Target:	End of the day **(P1)**	Average daily range **(P2)**	Other
Potential profit estimation:	N/A		
Profit probability evaluation:	Average		
Risks evaluation:	Average		
P/L ratio:	Neutral		
Potential advantages in favor of the open position:	N/A		
Possible complications, disadvantages, and risk warnings, and solutions to avoid them:	N/A		
Additional notices, recommendations, and trading tips:	Better when a position is open in the direction of the current medium-term trend. Also, some other reasons should support the idea of such a trade. However, if you trade on an intraday basis, the chance to make profit is quite acceptable. Can also be used for adding a position to another, profitable one.		

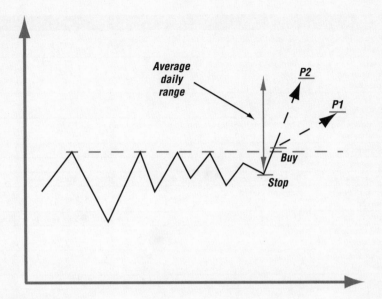

FIGURE 20.3a

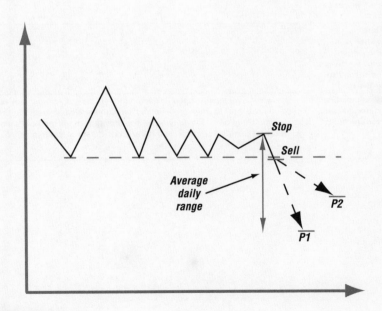

FIGURE 20.3b

Box 20.4			
Brief situation description:	A flat surface is formed on intraday charts.		
Currency recommended for a trade:	All majors and crosses.		
Trade characteristics:	Basic.		
Trade (entry point) suggestions:	Enter the market on the break of the formation.		
Entry time:	Any time.		
Entry execution:	Entry-stop order.		
Stop loss placed:	The opposite side of the day range.	Other technical level.	
Reverse if stops triggered:	Recommended.		
Target:	End of the day **(P1)**	Average daily range **(P2)**	Other
Potential profit estimation:	N/A		
Profit probability evaluation:	Average		
Risks evaluation:	Average		
P/L ratio:	Neutral		
Potential advantages in favor of the open position:	N/A		
Possible complications, disadvantages, and risk warnings, and solutions to avoid them:	N/A		
Additional notices, recommendations, and trading tips:	Better when a position is open in the direction of the current move. Usually supports the view that the move in this direction will happen during the day. If you trade on an intraday basis, the chance to make profit is quite acceptable. Can also be used for adding a position to another, profitable one.		

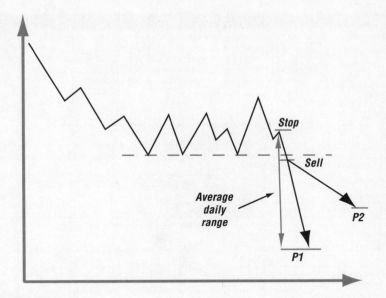

FIGURE 20.4a

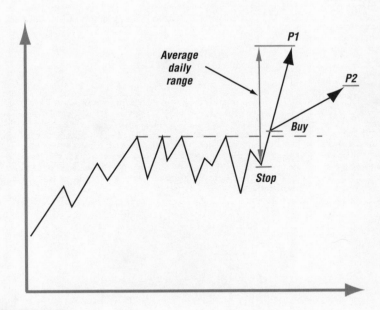

FIGURE 20.4b

Box 20.5			
Brief situation description:	The market approaches the major trendline drawn through two (or more) absolutely extreme points. (There should be the whole chart on one side from such a line and a totally free space on the other side.) **The trade can be executed only on the approach to a supportive line of the uptrend or at the resisting line of a downtrend.**		
Currency recommended for a trade:	All majors and crosses.		
Trade characteristics:	Basic.		
Trade (entry point) suggestions:	Enter the market 5 to 10 pips before the line in the direction, opposite to the direction of the move.		
Entry time:	Any time.		
Entry execution:	Limit or market order.		
Stop loss placed:	Behind the line.		
Reverse if stops triggered:	Recommended. (Trailing stop can also be used.)		
Target:	End of the day **(P1)**	Average daily range **(P2)**	Other technical point or reason
Potential profit estimation:	N/A		
Profit probability evaluation:	Above average		
Risks evaluation:	Below average		
P/L ratio:	Positive		
Potential advantages in favor of the open position:	N/A		
Possible complications, disadvantages, and risk warnings, and solutions to avoid them:	N/A		
Additional notices, recommendations, and trading tips:	The bigger the number of points lying on such a line, the less the probability to commit a profitable trade. I prefer to trade this template on the third or (at the maximum) fourth approach to the line. In the case of the fourth approach, I usually take profit early, using some market's hesitation ahead of the line.		

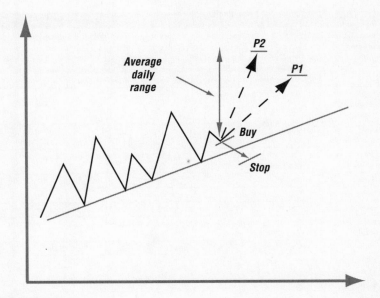

FIGURE 20.5a

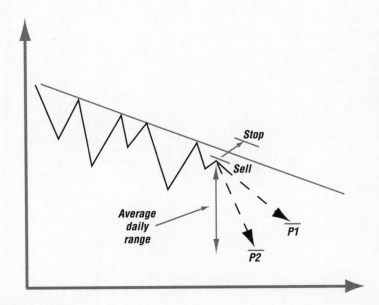

FIGURE 20.5b

Box 20.6

Brief situation description:	The market breaks the major trendline drawn through three or more absolutely extreme points. (There should be the whole chart on one side from such a line and a totally free space on the other side.) **The trade can be executed only on the approach to a supportive line of the uptrend or at the resisting line of a downtrend.**		
Currency recommended for a trade:	All majors and crosses.		
Trade characteristics:	Basic.		
Trade (entry point) suggestions:	Enter the market 5 to 10 pips at the break of the line in the direction of the move.		
Entry time:	Any time.		
Entry execution:	Entry-stop order.		
Stop loss placed:	The opposite side of the day range	Other technical level	
Reverse if stops triggered:	Recommended. (Trailing stops can be used also.)		
Target:	End of the day **(P1)**	Average daily range **(P2)**	Other technical point
Potential profit estimation:	N/A		
Profit probability evaluation:	Above average		
Risks evaluation:	Below average		
P/L ratio:	Positive		
Potential advantages in favor of the open position:	N/A		
Possible complications, disadvantages, and risk warnings, and solutions to avoid them:	N/A		
Additional notices, recommendations, and trading tips:	The bigger the number of points lying on such a line, the less the probability to commit a profitable trade. I prefer to trade this template on the fourth or larger approach to the line. The position can also be turned into a longer-term positional trade, because the break of such a line indicates the possibility of a trend change.		

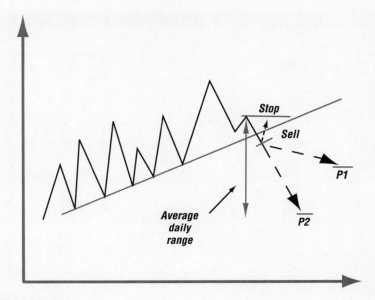

FIGURE 20.6a

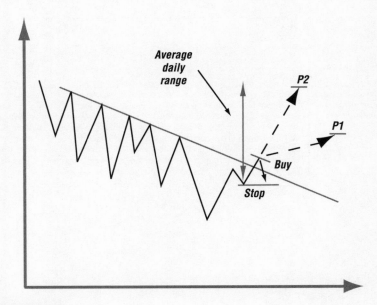

FIGURE 20.6b

Box 20.7

Brief situation description:	There is a CB intervention to support an undervalued currency in progress.
Currency recommended for a trade:	The undervalued currency and all its crosses.
Trade characteristics:	Trade of opportunity.
Trade (entry point) suggestions:	Enter the market on the run in the direction of the move using entry stops.
Entry time:	Any time.
Entry execution:	Entry-stop order.
Stop loss placed:	The opposite side of the day range / Other technical level
Reverse if stops triggered:	Not recommended.
Target:	End of the day **(P1)** / Other technical point **(P2)** / 100–300 pips **(P3)**
Potential profit estimation:	100 pips and up
Profit probability evaluation:	Very high
Risks evaluation:	Very low
P/L ratio:	Positive
Potential advantages in favor of the open position:	N/A
Possible complications, disadvantages, and risk warnings, and solutions to avoid them:	N/A
Additional notices, recommendations, and trading tips:	The intervention always takes place in support of an undervalued currency. Because it always goes against the trend and the most current move in exchange rates, it would be logical to start a trade by placing entry stops above the current day high as soon as the market price moves down 50 to 60 pips from it. Then, on the way down, a trailing stop can be used. It has to trail the market 60 to 100 pips above the most current low. After the intervention has begun and is confirmed, a trailing stop can be used to assure the profit and protect from unexpected losses.

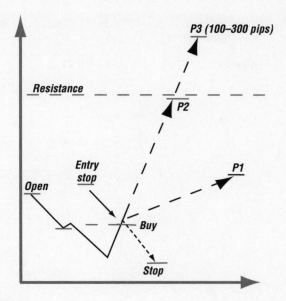

FIGURE 20.7a

CHAPTER 21

A Sample Trade

I have to admit that I was not going to write a conclusion to Part V or to the book in general. However, there was a perfect and recent sample taken from the real market that clearly illustrates the potential and the power of the templates just described, as well as some other thoughts and ideas about my common sense trading technique. I believe the real market situation shown in Figure 21.1 will give you clearer understanding of when and how the trading ideas described in the book can be applied to real trading. As you see, this particular day not only provided several different trading opportunities, but also gave a trader a choice of which trading signal to accept and which to ignore, in accordance with his individual trading profile and preferences.

On the chart, the market has formed a narrow horizontal channel at the beginning of a trading day and during the Asian session. Then, it broke the upper border of the channel, creating the opportunity to use Box 19.2 and to enter the market in the direction of the break for a quick and relatively moderate profit. For a more conservative trader who did not want the risk of entering the market with the position where the profit should be taken fast, there was another opportunity to enter the market. In accordance with another trading scheme (see Box 18.3), you can enter the market because it was moving in just one direction from the open price. If this trading opportunity was also considered an inappropriate one at the moment, another trading opportunity would arise soon. Entering the market on the break of the low of the previous range was recommended in accordance with four (!) other different templates, Box 19.1, Box 18.2, Box 20.4, and even Box 18.1.

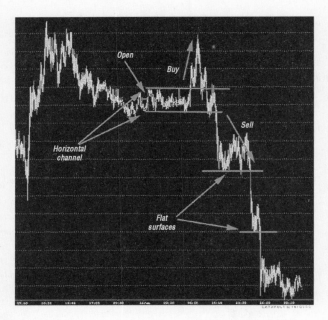

FIGURE 21.1

Then, the journey began, confirming several other thoughts and ideas described in the book.

First of all, on the way down, the market has formed at least three flat bottoms, and each of them was a clue for a trader that the move in this direction most likely would continue.

Second, as you can see, the idea of never opening a position against the main move of the day has also been confirmed, because the bottom pickers most likely were wiped out from the market by its powerful move. Because no major support or trendline was on the market's way during this day, a trade against the main move of the day would never pay off. It is important to remember that under similar circumstances it is usually very difficult (even close to impossible) to choose the right moment when the market may turn to the opposite direction. If you missed all the previous trading signals and opportunities, it would be better to stay away from the market, waiting for another trading day, than to take chances on picking a bottom without having a trading signal in favor of such an attempt.

Third, it is not really important where a position was entered and profit was actually taken. In any case, if during that day the trading strategy has been chosen in accordance with one or another template, the profit was unavoidable and would have ranged from 70 to 80 pips and up to a couple of hundred pips. However, the real importance of the example is the fact that this particular trading day can be considered as typical for the market. Its behavioral pattern was a common one and seen frequently (with some unimportant variations, of course). Using the templates provides a perfect opportunity to trade with no stress, and without the necessity of predicting the future or making forecasts in advance. A simple reaction in accordance with trading signals and basic techniques described in trading templates would do the job perfectly and would give a trader a great advantage against any other way of trading.

Index